# AUSTRALIA BY RAIL TRAVEL GUIDE 2025-2026

BY

Rune Greyhound

**Copyright Notice**
© 2025 [Rune Greyhound]. All rights reserved.

This document is protected by copyright law, and no part of it may be reproduced, stored in a retrieval system, or transmitted in any form—electronic, mechanical, photocopying, scanning, faxing, or otherwise—without prior written permission from the publisher or author. Unauthorized use of this material is strictly prohibited.

**A Note to Our Readers**

Welcome, fellow traveler! Before we plunge into this guide, I wanted to take a moment to address something important: while you won't find any images or maps included here, rest assured that every effort has been made to provide vivid descriptions and helpful information to bring your journey to life. Think of this as an invitation to explore with your imagination—and perhaps even discover new perspectives along the way.

My goal is simple: to equip you with everything you need to create unforgettable experiences on your travels, tailored to your own unique interests and preferences. Whether you're seeking hidden gems, cultural insights, or practical tips, my hope is that you'll find inspiration within these pages to craft adventures that resonate deeply with you.

# Table of Contents

**Acknowledgments**   10
**Dedication**   13
**Chapter 1: Introduction – Welcome Aboard!**   14
   1.1 Why Take the Train? Discovering Australia Through Its Rails   14
   1.2 What Makes Rail Travel Unique in Australia   15
   1.3 History of Australia   17
   1.4 Atmosphere Conditions   18
   1.5 Currency and Money Matters   19
   1.6 Who This Book Is For (And How to Use It)   20

**Chapter 2: All About Australian Railways**   22
   2.1 A Brief History of Trains in Australia   22
   2.2 Types of Trains You'll Encounter   24
   2.3 Luxury Trains vs. Budget-Friendly Options   25
   2.4 Scenic Routes vs. Urban Commuter Lines   26
   2.5 Understanding the Railway Network: Key Operators and Services   28

**Chapter 3: Iconic Train Journeys Across Australia** 31
   3.1 The Ghan: From Adelaide to Darwin – The Ultimate Outback Adventure   31
   3.2 Indian Pacific: Coast-to-Coast Magic Between

    Sydney and Perth    33
    3.3 Spirit of Queensland: Tropical Beauty from Brisbane to Cairns    34
    3.4 Overland: Melbourne to Adelaide – Wine Country and Beyond    35
    3.5 Savannahlander: Off-the-Beaten-Path Exploration in Far North Queensland    36
    3.6 Other Notable Routes Worth Exploring    38

**Chapter 4: Planning Your Rail Journey**    40
    4.1 Step-by-Step Guide to Booking Tickets    40
    4.2 Online Reservations vs. Travel Agencies    42
    4.3 Discounts, Deals, and Packages    43
    4.4 When to Go: Best Seasons for Each Route    43
    4.5 Budgeting for Your Trip: Costs Breakdown    45
    4.6 Accommodation Classes (Platinum, Gold, Economy)    45
    4.7 Food and Beverage Expenses Onboard    46
    4.8 Packing Essentials for Long Train Rides    47
    4.9 How to Connect From Neighboring Countries    48
    4.10 Seven-Day Sample Itinerary    49

**Chapter 5: Life on the Rails**    50
    5.1 What to Expect During Your Journey    50
    5.2 Sleeping Comfortably in Cabins or Seats    51
    5.3 Dining Cars and Meals on Board    53
    5.4 Entertainment and Activities While Traveling    54
    5.5 Tips for Staying Entertained: Books, Podcasts, Games, and More    55
    5.6 Navigating Time Zones and Long Distances    56

**Chapter 6: Culinary Delights Along the Rails**    59

6.1 Savoring Regional Cuisine Onboard 59
6.2 Highlights from The Ghan's Outback Dinners 60
6.3 Fine Dining on Indian Pacific: Multi-Course Menus with Local Ingredients 61
6.4 Casual Eats on Spirit of Queensland: Fresh Seafood and Tropics-Inspired Dishes 61
6.5 Must-Try Foods at Major Stops 62
6.6 Oysters in Coffin Bay (The Ghan) 63
6.7 Barossa Valley Wines (Indian Pacific) 64
6.8 Tropical Fruits in Cairns (Spirit of Queensland) 64
6.9 Special Dietary Needs: Vegan, Vegetarian, and Gluten-Free Options 65

**Chapter 7: Accommodations Options Near Train Stations** 67

7.1 Luxury Hotels Close to Major Stations 67
7.2 Boutique Stays in Sydney, Melbourne, and Perth 68
7.3 Desert Resorts in Alice Springs and Darwin 69
7.4 Budget-Friendly Hostels and Guesthouses 70
7.5 Unique Lodging Experiences 71
7.6 Glamping Under the Stars Near Uluru 72
7.7 Heritage Cottages in Historic Towns Like Broken Hill 73
7.8 Tips for Booking Last-Minute Stays During Peak Seasons 74

**Chapter 8: Transportation Beyond Trains** 76

8.1 Navigating Cities and Regions After Disembarking 76
8.2 Public Transit Systems in Major Cities 77
8.3 Renting Cars for Road Trips Around Regional

    Areas    78
    8.4 Guided Tours and Shuttles for Day Excursions 80
    8.5 Connecting Flights for International Travelers  80
    8.6 Cycling and Walking Trails for Eco-Conscious Adventurers    81

**Chapter 9: Exploring Major Cities in Australia by Rail**    84
    9.1 Sydney: Coastal Charm and Urban Energy    84
    9.2 Melbourne: Culture, Cafés, and Hidden Laneways    85
    9.3 Brisbane: Gateway to Sunshine and Surf    86
    9.4 Adelaide: Wine Country and Festivals Galore    87
    9.5 Perth: Modern Meets Natural Beauty    88
    9.6 Cairns: Tropical Paradise and Reef Adventures    89
    9.7 Darwin: Outback Vibes and Indigenous Culture    91
    9.8 Alice Springs: Heart of the Red Centre    92

**Chapter 10: Scenic Highlights Along the Way**    94
    10.1 Must-See Landscapes from Your Window    94
    10.2 Red Deserts of Central Australia    95
    10.3 Lush Rainforests of Tropical Queensland    96
    10.4 Vast Plains of the Nullarbor    97
    10.5 Wildlife Spotting Opportunities    98
    10.6 Sunrise and Sunset Moments Over Iconic Terrain    98

**Chapter 11: Off-Train Adventures**    101
    11.1 Making the Most of Stopovers and Excursions    101
    11.2 Top Stops on The Ghan: Alice Springs,

Katherine Gorge, Uluru 102
11.3 Indian Pacific Highlights: Broken Hill, Kalgoorlie, Avon Valley 104
11.4 Spirit of Queensland Gems: Daintree Rainforest, Great Barrier Reef 105
11.5 Guided Tours vs. Independent Exploration 106
11.6 Short Detours for Nature Lovers, Foodies, and History Buffs 107

**Chapter 12: Cultural Connections** 110
12.1 Learning About Indigenous Australia Through Rail Travel 110
12.2 Sacred Sites and Stories Along the Tracks 111
12.3 Respectful Engagement with Local Communities 112
12.4 Meeting Fellow Travelers and Sharing Stories 113
12.5 Celebrating Regional Cultures Through Food, Art, and Festivals 114

**Chapter 13: Photography and Journaling on the Rails** 117
13.1 Capturing Stunning Photos from Moving Trains 117
13.2 Camera Settings for Shooting Through Windows 118
13.3 Best Times of Day for Landscape Shots 119
13.4 Keeping a Travel Journal: Reflecting on Your Journey 120
13.5 Creating Memories That Last: Souvenirs and Keepsakes 121

**Chapter 14: Insider Tips for First-Time Rail Travelers** 123

14.1 Train Etiquette: Dos and Don'ts for a Smooth Ride — 123
14.2 Handling Challenges: Delays, Connectivity Issues, and More — 125
14.3 Staying Healthy and Comfortable on Long Journeys — 126
14.4 Connecting with Locals and Making Friends — 127

**Chapter 15: Sustainable Travel by Rail** — 129
15.1 Why Trains Are an Eco-Friendly Choice — 129
15.2 Supporting Local Economies Through Rail Tourism — 130
15.3 Reducing Your Carbon Footprint While Exploring Australia — 131

**Chapter 16: Appendices** — 134
16.1 Appendix A: Apps, Websites, and Resources — 134
16.2 Appendix B: Glossary of Train and Rail Terminology — 136
16.3 Appendix C: Glossary of Local Phrases — 136
16.4 Appendix D: Detailed Maps of Major Train Routes — 137
16.5 Appendix E: Contact Information for Booking Operators and Emergency Contact Numbers — 138
16.6 Appendix F: Glossary of Rail Travel Terms — 139
16.7 Appendix G: Checklist for Planning Your Rail Adventure — 140

**Chapter 17: Index** — 142
**Chapter 18: Conclusion: All Aboard for Adventure** — 149

## Acknowledgments

This book would not have been possible without the collective inspiration, expertise, and support of so many individuals and communities who share a deep love for Australia and its railways. To each of them, I extend my heartfelt gratitude.

First and foremost, I'd like to thank the countless travelers whose stories, photographs, and experiences brought this guide to life. Your passion for exploration and your willingness to embrace the magic of train travel inspired every page. Special thanks go to those who shared personal anecdotes about their journeys—from dining under starlit skies aboard The Ghan to marveling at sunrise over Uluru—your voices are woven into the fabric of this book.

To the dedicated teams at Journey Beyond Rail Expeditions, Queensland Rail Travel, NSW TrainLink, and other operators: thank you for opening doors (and tracks!) to unforgettable adventures. Your commitment to preserving Australia's natural beauty while offering world-class hospitality is nothing short of remarkable.

I'm also deeply grateful to the Indigenous custodians of the land, whose rich cultural heritage shapes the very essence of Australia. Thank you for allowing us to learn from your traditions, hear your Dreamtime stories, and appreciate the sacred sites along these rail routes. This book strives to honor your legacy with respect and admiration.

A special note of appreciation goes to the local artisans, chefs, guides, and small business owners whose creativity and hard work enrich every stop along the way. From Barossa Valley winemakers to Daintree Rainforest rangers, your contributions remind us that travel is as much about people as it is about places.

Behind the scenes, I owe immense gratitude to researchers, cartographers, photographers, and writers whose work has illuminated Australia's landscapes and history. Their insights helped shape the detailed maps, glossaries, and practical tips included in this guide.

Finally, to my family, friends, and colleagues—you've been unwavering sources of encouragement throughout this project. Your belief in the power of storytelling and sustainable travel kept me motivated on even the longest days. And to readers like you, thank you for choosing to commence on this journey with me. It is my hope that this book serves as both a trusted companion and a source of inspiration for your own Australian rail adventure.

Here's to trains, trails, and timeless memories—may they carry you far beyond where the tracks end.

Thank you all from the bottom of my heart.

# Dedication

This book is dedicated to those who find joy in the journey, beauty in the landscape, and meaning in the moments that unfold along the way.

To the quiet strength of steel tracks stretching across Australia's vast expanse, binding cities, deserts, rainforests, and coastlines into a single, breathtaking narrative.

To the people who make these journeys unforgettable—the guides sharing their knowledge, the chefs crafting regional flavors, the artisans preserving traditions, and the fellow travelers whose stories remind us we're all connected by shared experiences.

And to you, dear reader—curious, adventurous, and open-hearted—may this guide be your companion as you explore the rich treasures of Australia by rail. May it inspire you to see beyond the window, embrace the unexpected, and carry home memories that will last a lifetime.

## Chapter 1: Introduction – Welcome Aboard!

Welcome to the ultimate guide for exploring Australia by rail! Whether you're dreaming of an epic adventure through the Outback, a luxurious journey across vast landscapes, or simply a relaxing way to see this incredible country, this book is your ticket to making it happen. Let's plunge into everything you need to know before commencing on your Australian rail odyssey.

### 1.1 Why Take the Train? Discovering Australia Through Its Rails

Australia is a land of extremes—vast deserts, lush rainforests, rugged coastlines, and bustling cities. While planes get you there quickly and cars offer flexibility, trains provide something truly special: time. Time to slow down, soak in the scenery, and connect with the heart of the country.

Imagine sipping coffee as the golden sun rises over the Nullarbor Plain, spotting kangaroos hopping alongside the tracks, or enjoying gourmet meals inspired by regional flavors—all without worrying about driving or navigating. Trains let you experience Australia at its most authentic, taking you deep into remote areas that are often inaccessible by other means.

For many travelers, train journeys aren't just transportation—they're destinations in themselves. The rhythm of the rails, the ever-changing views outside your window, and the camaraderie among fellow passengers create memories that last a lifetime. So why take the train? Because it's not just about getting from point A to B; it's about the journey becoming part of the story.

## 1.2 What Makes Rail Travel Unique in Australia

Rail travel in Australia stands apart for several reasons:

- Scenic Beauty: Few places in the world can rival Australia's multiple landscapes, and trains give you front-row seats to these wonders. From the red sands of the Outback to the tropical greenery of Queensland, every route offers breathtaking vistas.

- Comfort and Convenience: Unlike cramped airplane seats or long hours behind the wheel, trains allow you to stretch out, relax, and enjoy the ride. Many luxury services even include private cabins, fine dining, and panoramic windows.

- Cultural Immersion: Train routes often pass through small towns and Indigenous lands, giving you a glimpse into the local culture and history. Off-train excursions let you explore iconic landmarks like Uluru or the Great Barrier Reef.

- Eco-Friendly Travel: Trains have a much smaller carbon footprint compared to planes or cars. By choosing rail travel, you're supporting sustainable tourism while still experiencing all the wonders Australia has to offer.

In short, rail travel combines comfort, adventure, and sustainability—a perfect trifecta for discovering Australia!

## 1.3 History of Australia

To truly appreciate Australia, it helps to understand its rich history. This ancient land has been inhabited by Aboriginal peoples for over 65,000 years, making it home to one of the oldest continuous cultures in the world. Their deep connection to the land is reflected in the stories, art, and traditions passed down through generations.

European exploration began in the 17th century, but it wasn't until 1788 that British settlers established a penal colony in Sydney Cove. Over time, waves of immigration transformed Australia into the multicultural nation it is today. Railways played a crucial role in this transformation, connecting far-flung regions and opening up opportunities for trade, mining, and agriculture.

The first railway line opened in 1854 between Melbourne and Port Melbourne, marking the beginning of Australia's rail network. Today, modern trains carry millions of passengers annually, blending cutting-edge technology with the romance of old-world travel.

Understanding this historical context adds depth to your journey. As you glide through the Outback or along coastal routes, imagine the pioneers who once traversed these same paths—and how their legacy shapes the Australia we see today.

## 1.4 Atmosphere Conditions

Australia's climate varies dramatically depending on where you are, so it's important to prepare accordingly. Here's a quick overview of what to expect:

- Desert Regions (e.g., Central Australia): Hot during the day and surprisingly cold at night. Bring layers, sunscreen, and plenty of water if you plan to explore off-train stops like Alice Springs or Uluru.

- Tropical North (e.g., Queensland): Humid and warm year-round, with wet seasons from November to April. Pack lightweight clothing, insect repellent, and rain gear.

- Southern Cities (e.g., Sydney, Melbourne): Temperate climates with four distinct seasons. Winters (June–August) can be chilly, especially in Melbourne, while summers (December–February) bring heatwaves.

- Coastal Areas: Generally mild and pleasant, though beware of strong winds near cliffs or beaches.

Keep an eye on weather forecasts before your trip, and adjust your packing list based on the regions you'll visit. Most train carriages are air-conditioned, so you'll stay comfortable onboard regardless of the conditions outside.

## 1.5 Currency and Money Matters

Australia uses the Australian Dollar (AUD), symbolized as $ or AUD. Here's what you need to know about handling money during your travels:

- Cash vs. Cards: Credit and debit cards are widely accepted in cities and larger towns, but cash may be necessary in remote areas or smaller businesses. ATMs are available at most stations and towns along major routes.

- Currency Exchange: If you're bringing foreign currency, exchange it at banks, airports, or authorized exchange offices. Avoid exchanging money at hotels or tourist spots, as rates tend to be less favorable.

- Budgeting Tips: Train tickets can range from affordable economy seats to premium luxury cabins. Research costs in advance and factor in extras like meals, excursions, and accommodations near stations.

- Tipping Etiquette: Tipping isn't mandatory in Australia, but it's appreciated for exceptional service. In restaurants, rounding up the bill or leaving 10% is common practice.

Pro Tip: Notify your bank before traveling to avoid issues with international transactions, and consider carrying a mix of cash and cards for convenience.

## 1.6 Who This Book Is For (And How to Use It)

This book is designed for anyone eager to explore Australia by rail, whether you're a first-time visitor or a seasoned traveler looking to try something new. Here's how to make the most of it:

- Newbies: Start with Chapters 1–3 to familiarize yourself with rail travel basics, planning tips, and must-know information about Australia.

- Adventure Seekers: Plunge into Chapters 5–8 for detailed insights into scenic highlights, culinary delights, and off-train adventures.

- Luxury Travelers: Focus on sections about premium services like The Ghan and Indian Pacific, which offer unparalleled comfort and elegance.

-Budget-Conscious Explorers: Look for advice on affordable options, discounts, and free activities throughout the book.

Use this guide as your go-to resource for planning and inspiration. Highlight key sections, jot down notes, and refer back to it whenever you need guidance. Remember, the goal is to enjoy the journey—not stress over logistics. We've got you covered every step of the way!

Congratulations—you're officially ready to commence on your Australian rail adventure! Keep reading to discover the iconic train routes, practical tips, and hidden gems that await you. All aboard!

## Chapter 2: All About Australian Railways

Australia's railways are more than just a mode of transport—they're an integral part of the country's history, culture, and modern identity. This chapter will introduce you to the fascinating world of Australian railways, from their humble beginnings to the state-of-the-art services available today. Whether you're dreaming of luxury cabins or practical commuter lines, this guide will help you understand what to expect when traveling by train in Australia.

## 2.1 A Brief History of Trains in Australia

Railways have played a pivotal role in shaping Australia into the nation it is today. The first railway line opened in 1854 between Melbourne and Port Melbourne, marking the start of an era that would revolutionize transportation across the continent. Over the decades, rail networks expanded rapidly, connecting cities, rural towns, and remote regions.

- Colonial Beginnings: In the mid-19th century, railways were built primarily to support growing industries like agriculture, mining, and manufacturing. Each colony developed its own system, leading to differences in track gauges (the width between rails). These inconsistencies made interstate travel challenging until standardization efforts began in the 20th century.

- The Gold Rush Era: The discovery of gold in the 1850s spurred rapid railway expansion as miners and settlers flocked to regional areas. Towns sprang up along rail lines, transforming isolated landscapes into thriving communities.

- Transcontinental Connections: By the early 20th century, ambitious projects like the Trans-Australian Railway linked Perth with Adelaide, bridging the vast Nullarbor Plain. Later, routes like The Ghan connected the southern coast to Darwin, opening up access to the Outback.

Today, Australia boasts one of the largest rail networks in the world, covering over 33,000 kilometers. Modern trains combine cutting-edge technology with the timeless charm of rail travel, offering unforgettable experiences for passengers.

## 2.2 Types of Trains You'll Encounter

Australia's rail network caters to a wide variety of travelers, from urban commuters to adventurous tourists. Here are the main types of trains you'll encounter:

-Long-Distance Trains: Designed for extended journeys, these trains connect major cities and remote regions. Examples include The Ghan, Indian Pacific, and Spirit of Queensland. They often feature sleeper cabins, dining cars, and panoramic windows.

- Regional Trains: These operate within states or territories, serving smaller towns and rural areas. While less luxurious than long-distance options, they provide affordable and convenient access to regional attractions.

- Urban Commuter Lines: Found in major cities like Sydney, Melbourne, and Brisbane, these trains are ideal for short trips within metropolitan areas. They're fast, frequent, and budget-friendly.

- Tourist Trains: Specialized services like the Savannahlander and Puffing Billy offer unique experiences, focusing on sightseeing and cultural immersion rather than speed or efficiency.

Understanding the type of train you'll be traveling on helps set expectations for comfort, amenities, and overall experience.

## 2.3 Luxury Trains vs. Budget-Friendly Options

When planning your rail journey, one of the first decisions you'll need to make is whether to splurge on luxury or opt for a budget-friendly option. Both have their merits, depending on your preferences and priorities.

**Luxury Trains**
- What to Expect: Think first-class cabins, gourmet meals prepared by top chefs, attentive staff, and breathtaking views through oversized windows.
Examples:
-The Ghan: Known for its opulent accommodations and immersive Outback excursions.
- Indian Pacific: Offers platinum service with spacious suites and exclusive off-train experiences.
- Spirit of Queensland: Combines sleek design with comfortable RailBed seating for overnight journeys.

- Best For: Travelers seeking indulgence, relaxation, and once-in-a-lifetime memories.

**Budget-Friendly Options**
- What to Expect: Economy seating, shared facilities, and fewer onboard luxuries—but still plenty of charm and adventure.
- Examples:
- Overland: Connects Melbourne and Adelaide at an affordable price.
- Queensland Rail's Tilt Train: Fast and efficient, perfect for travelers watching their wallet.
- Regional Services: Operated by state governments, these trains are economical ways to explore local areas.
- Best For: Backpackers, families, and anyone prioritizing value over extravagance.

No matter which option you choose, every train ride offers a chance to witness Australia's stunning landscapes and vibrant culture.

## 2.4 Scenic Routes vs. Urban Commuter Lines

Australia's rail network includes two distinct categories of routes: scenic routes designed for leisure and exploration, and urban commuter lines focused on daily transportation needs.

Scenic Routes
- Characteristics: Slow-paced, picturesque, and packed with opportunities for sightseeing. These routes showcase Australia's natural beauty and iconic landmarks.
Examples:
- The Ghan: Takes you through the heart of the Outback, stopping at Alice Springs and Katherine.
- Indian Pacific: Crosses three time zones and passes through the Nullarbor Plain and Blue Mountains.
- Savannahlander: Winds through tropical savannahs and historic mining towns in Queensland.
- Highlights: Panoramic windows, guided excursions, and stops at must-see destinations.

Urban Commuter Lines
-Characteristics: Fast, frequent, and functional. These trains serve busy city centers and suburbs, providing reliable public transit for locals and visitors alike.
Examples:
- Sydney Trains: Covers Greater Sydney, including popular spots like Bondi Junction and Circular Quay.
- Melbourne Metro: Features a free City Loop tram zone and easy connections to regional Victoria.

- Brisbane Network: Includes ferries, buses, and trains for seamless inner-city travel.
- Highlights: Convenience, affordability, and integration with other forms of public transport.

If your goal is to soak in the scenery, prioritize scenic routes. For quick city hops or commuting, stick to urban lines.

## 2.5 Understanding the Railway Network: Key Operators and Services

Navigating Australia's rail system can seem daunting at first, but knowing the key players makes it much easier. Below are the primary operators and the services they provide:

- Journey Beyond Rail Expeditions:
- Operates iconic long-distance trains like The Ghan, Indian Pacific, and Great Southern.
- Focuses on luxury travel, offering all-inclusive packages with meals, accommodations, and excursions.

- Queensland Rail:

- Manages regional and tourist trains within Queensland, including the Spirit of Queensland and Tilt Train.
- Provides affordable and efficient connections to coastal destinations and inland towns.

- NSW TrainLink:
- Connects New South Wales and neighboring states via regional and intercity services.
- Ideal for exploring areas like the Blue Mountains, Hunter Valley, and Canberra.

- V/Line (Victoria):
- Runs regional trains and coaches throughout Victoria, linking Melbourne with Geelong, Ballarat, Bendigo, and beyond.
- Great for day trips or weekend getaways.

- Transwa (Western Australia):
- Offers long-distance bus and train services across WA, including the Prospector route between Perth and Kalgoorlie.
- Perfect for adventurers heading to the wild west.

- Metro Systems (Urban Networks):
- Each capital city has its own metro system managed by local authorities. Examples include Sydney Trains, Melbourne Metro, and Brisbane's CityTrain network.

- These systems are essential for navigating urban environments efficiently.

**Pro Tip: Always check the operator's website for schedules, ticket prices, and special promotions before booking your trip.**

**With this overview of Australian railways, you're now equipped to navigate the country's multiple rail offerings. Whether you're chasing luxury, affordability, or pure adventure, there's a train—and a route—perfectly suited to your needs.**

## Chapter 3: Iconic Train Journeys Across Australia

Australia's railways offer some of the most breathtaking and unforgettable journeys in the world. From coast-to-coast crossings to tropical adventures, these iconic routes showcase the country's multiple landscapes, rich history, and vibrant culture. In this chapter, we'll take you through six legendary train journeys that define Australian rail travel—and introduce a few hidden gems worth exploring.

## 3.1 The Ghan: From Adelaide to Darwin – The Ultimate Outback Adventure

**Overview:**
The Ghan is more than just a train—it's an institution. Named after the Afghan cameleers who once traversed the harsh Australian interior, this iconic route spans 2,979 kilometers (1,851 miles) from Adelaide in the south to Darwin in the north. It's a true Outback odyssey, taking you through the heart of Australia's red desert, ancient gorges, and lush tropical regions.

Highlights:
- Alice Springs: Explore the spiritual heart of Australia, home to Uluru (Ayers Rock), Kata Tjuta (The Olgas), and the Royal Flying Doctor Service Museum.
- Katherine Gorge: Discover Nitmiluk National Park with optional excursions like river cruises or helicopter flights over the stunning gorge system.
- Outback Sunsets: Watch as golden hues transform the arid landscape into a surreal masterpiece.

Onboard Experience:
- Choose between Platinum Service (luxurious cabins with ensuite bathrooms) or Gold Service (comfortable sleeper berths with shared facilities).
- Indulge in regionally inspired meals featuring native ingredients like kangaroo, barramundi, and quandong.
- Attend onboard storytelling sessions about Indigenous culture and the history of the Outback.

Why Take This Journey?
The Ghan is perfect for adventurers seeking solitude, jaw-dropping scenery, and a deep connection to Australia's rugged soul.

## 3.2 Indian Pacific: Coast-to-Coast Magic Between Sydney and Perth

**Overview:**
Spanning 4,352 kilometers (2,704 miles), the Indian Pacific links Australia's east and west coasts in style. This transcontinental marvel takes four days to complete its journey, crossing three time zones and countless landscapes—from urban skylines to endless deserts.

**Highlights:**
- Blue Mountains: Marvel at dramatic cliffs, eucalyptus forests, and cascading waterfalls just outside Sydney.
- Broken Hill: Visit the "Silver City," known for its mining heritage and vibrant art scene.
- Nullarbor Plain: Traverse one of the world's largest stretches of flat, treeless land—a surreal experience unlike any other.
- Avon Valley: End your journey near Perth with picturesque views of rolling hills and quaint villages.

**Onboard Experience:**
- Opt for Platinum Service (private cabins with panoramic windows) or Gold Service (sleeper berths with access to dining cars).

- Enjoy multi-course meals paired with premium Australian wines.
- Participate in off-train excursions like wine tastings in Barossa Valley or stargazing in the Outback.

Why Take This Journey?
The Indian Pacific offers a mix of luxury, adventure, and cultural immersion, making it ideal for travelers who want to see the breadth of Australia in comfort.

## 3.3 Spirit of Queensland: Tropical Beauty from Brisbane to Cairns

Overview:
For those craving sun, sand, and rainforests, the Spirit of Queensland delivers. This 1,681-kilometer (1,044-mile) journey hugs Australia's northeastern coastline, showcasing tropical paradise from start to finish.

Highlights:
- **Sunshine Coast:** Relax in beachside towns like Noosa and Mooloolaba before continuing north.
- **Townsville:** Plunge into Great Barrier Reef adventures or explore Magnetic Island.
- **Cairns:** Gateway to the reef, Daintree Rainforest, and Kuranda Scenic Railway.

**Onboard Experience:**
- Travel in comfort with RailBed seating, which converts into a lie-flat bed for overnight legs.
- Sample fresh seafood and tropical fruits inspired by Queensland's bounty.
- Gaze out at turquoise waters and verdant mountains through large picture windows.

**Why Take This Journey?**
This route is perfect for nature lovers, snorkelers, and anyone wanting to soak up Australia's tropical charm.

## 3.4 Overland: Melbourne to Adelaide – Wine Country and Beyond

**Overview:**
Though shorter than other routes, the Overland packs plenty of charm into its 8-hour journey between Melbourne and Adelaide. Known for affordability and convenience, it's a favorite among budget-conscious travelers.

**Highlights:**
- Grampians National Park: Stop en route to hike scenic trails and spot wildlife.

- Barossa Valley: Detour to sample world-class wines from Penfolds, Jacob's Creek, and other renowned vineyards.
- Coorong National Park: Near Adelaide, enjoy bird watching and kayaking in pristine wetlands.

Onboard Experience:
- Economy seating provides basic comfort, while Red Premium upgrades offer extra legroom and complimentary snacks.
- Chat with fellow passengers and share stories of your travels.

Why Take This Journey?
Ideal for short trips, the Overland combines affordability with easy access to South Australia's famous wine regions.

## 3.5 Savannahlander: Off-the-Beaten-Path Exploration in Far North Queensland

Overview:
The Savannahlander is a unique, self-guided adventure that takes you deep into Queensland's untamed wilderness. Operating weekly, this 4-day expedition departs from Cairns and ventures into

remote cattle stations, historic mining towns, and savannah woodlands.

Highlights:
- Undara Lava Tubes: Explore ancient volcanic caves formed 190,000 years ago.
- Cobbold Gorge: Paddle through narrow sandstone walls on guided boat tours.
- Gulf Savanna: Experience the vastness of northern Australia, where cattle roam freely under endless skies.

Onboard Experience:
- Travel aboard a vintage railmotor, a retro-style vehicle blending nostalgia with practicality.
- Stay in charming lodges or camp under the stars during overnight stops.
- Meet local characters and learn about life in rural Australia.

Why Take This Journey?
If you're looking for something truly offbeat and immersive, the Savannahlander promises authenticity and adventure.

## 3.6 Other Notable Routes Worth Exploring

While the above journeys dominate Australia's rail scene, several lesser-known routes deserve attention:

- Puffing Billy Railway (Victoria): A heritage steam train winding through the Dandenong Ranges, offering family-friendly fun and stunning forest views.
- Kuranda Scenic Railway (Queensland): A short but spectacular ride through rainforests and waterfalls near Cairns.
- Prospector (Western Australia): Connects Perth and Kalgoorlie, passing through goldfields and wildflower country.
- XPT (New South Wales): Links Sydney with regional hubs like Dubbo, Armidale, and Casino, providing affordable access to inland NSW.

Each of these routes offers unique experiences, whether you're chasing history, nature, or quirky charm.

**Final Thoughts**

Australia's iconic train journeys are more than just transportation—they're gateways to discovery. Whether you're chasing luxury aboard The Ghan, marveling at the Nullarbor Plain on the Indian Pacific, or savoring tropical delights on the Spirit of Queensland, each route has its own story to tell.

# Chapter 4: Planning Your Rail Journey

Planning a rail journey through Australia might seem overwhelming at first, but with the right preparation, it can be smooth, stress-free, and even fun. This chapter will walk you through everything you need to know to book your tickets, choose the best time to travel, budget effectively, and pack like a pro. We'll also provide a sample itinerary to inspire your own adventure.

## 4.1 Step-by-Step Guide to Booking Tickets

Booking train tickets in Australia is straightforward if you follow these simple steps:

**1. Decide on Your Route:**
Choose the train route that aligns with your interests—whether it's The Ghan for Outback exploration or the Spirit of Queensland for tropical beauty.

**2. Check Schedules:**

Visit the official website of the train operator (e.g., Journey Beyond Rail Expeditions, Queensland Rail) to view departure dates and times.

**3. Select Accommodation Class:**
Decide between luxury options like Platinum Service or more budget-friendly Economy seating.

**4. Book Early:**
Train journeys, especially popular ones like The Ghan and Indian Pacific, fill up quickly. Book several months in advance to secure your spot.

**5. Add Extras (Optional):**
Many operators offer add-ons like off-train excursions, gourmet meals, or guided tours. Consider what enhances your experience.

**6. Confirm Payment:**
Use a secure payment method and ensure you receive a confirmation email with your e-ticket.

**7. Prepare for Departure:**
Double-check your booking details, print your ticket (if required), and arrive at the station at least 30 minutes before departure.

## 4.2 Online Reservations vs. Travel Agencies

When it comes to booking your rail journey, you have two main options: online reservations or working with a travel agency.

- Online Reservations:
- Pros: Convenient, often cheaper, and allows you to compare prices easily. You can book directly through the operator's website or third-party platforms.
-Cons: Requires self-research; no personalized assistance unless you contact customer support.

- Travel Agencies:
- Pros: Personalized service, expert advice, and potential access to exclusive deals or packages. Ideal for first-timers or those planning complex itineraries.
- Cons: May charge additional fees, and not all agencies specialize in Australian rail travel.

For tech-savvy travelers comfortable with DIY planning, online reservations are ideal. If you prefer hand-holding and insider tips, go with a trusted travel agent.

## 4.3 Discounts, Deals, and Packages

Train operators frequently offer discounts and bundled packages to make your journey more affordable. Here's how to save:

- Early Bird Discounts: Book months in advance to lock in lower rates.
- Senior/Student Discounts: Check eligibility requirements for reduced fares.
- Group Rates: Traveling with family or friends? Ask about group discounts.
- Seasonal Promotions: Look out for flash sales during shoulder seasons (spring and autumn).
- All-Inclusive Packages: Combine train tickets with accommodations, meals, and excursions for better value.

Pro Tip: Sign up for newsletters from operators like Journey Beyond Rail Expeditions to stay informed about special offers.

## 4.4 When to Go: Best Seasons for Each Route

Timing your trip wisely ensures optimal weather and fewer crowds. Here's a breakdown by region:

- The Ghan (Adelaide to Darwin):
- Best Time: April–October (dry season in the north, mild temperatures in the south).
- Avoid: November–March due to extreme heat and humidity in the Top End.

- Indian Pacific (Sydney to Perth):
- Best Time: March–May or September–November (mild weather across all zones).
- Avoid: Summer months (December–February) when the Nullarbor Plain gets scorching hot.

- Spirit of Queensland (Brisbane to Cairns):
- Best Time: May–September (cooler, drier conditions in the tropics).
- Avoid: Wet season (December–April) when heavy rains and cyclones occur.

- Overland (Melbourne to Adelaide):
- Best Time: Year-round, though spring (September–November) is particularly pleasant.

- Savannahlander (Cairns to Forsayth):
- Best Time: May–August (cool and dry weather in the Gulf region).

## 4.5 Budgeting for Your Trip: Costs Breakdown

Rail travel costs vary based on factors like route, class, and extras. Here's a rough estimate:

- Economy Seats: AUD $150–$300 per leg.
- Gold Service (Sleeper Berths): AUD $1,000–$2,500 per person, depending on the route.
- Platinum Service (Luxury Cabins): AUD $3,000–$6,000 per person.
- Food/Beverages: Included in higher classes; expect AUD $20–$50/day for Economy.
- Excursions: Off-train activities typically range from AUD $50–$200 each.

Factor in accommodation near stations, transportation beyond trains, and daily expenses like souvenirs and snacks.

## 4.6 Accommodation Classes (Platinum, Gold, Economy)

Most long-distance trains offer multiple accommodation tiers. Here's what to expect:

- Platinum Service:
- Private cabins with ensuite bathrooms, panoramic windows, and premium amenities.
- Best For: Luxury seekers wanting maximum comfort.

- Gold Service:
- Sleeper berths with shared facilities, cozy lounges, and included meals.
- Best For: Mid-range travelers balancing cost and comfort.

- Economy Class:
- Reclining seats with limited legroom; no overnight sleeping arrangements.
- Best For: Short trips or budget-conscious explorers.

Choose based on your priorities—luxury, affordability, or practicality.

## 4.7 Food and Beverage Expenses Onboard

Dining onboard is one of the highlights of Australian rail travel. Here's what to expect:

- Included Meals: Most Gold and Platinum services include breakfast, lunch, dinner, and snacks. Menus feature regional specialties like barramundi, kangaroo, and tropical fruits.
- Beverage Selection: Complimentary tea, coffee, soft drinks, beer, and wine are often provided.
- Economy Class: Bring your own food or purchase meals separately (AUD $10–$25 per item).

If dietary restrictions apply, notify the operator in advance to arrange suitable options.

## 4.8 Packing Essentials for Long Train Rides

Packing smart ensures comfort during your journey. Here's a checklist:

- Clothing: Layers for varying climates, sturdy shoes for excursions, and formal attire for dining (optional).
- Toiletries: Travel-sized items, sunscreen, insect repellent, and medications.
- Entertainment: Books, e-readers, headphones, playing cards, or journals.
- Tech Gear: Phone charger, power bank, camera, and adapter (Australia uses Type I plugs).

- Snacks: Non-perishable treats for Economy passengers.
- Miscellaneous: Eye mask, earplugs, reusable water bottle, and cash for small purchases.

## 4.9 How to Connect From Neighboring Countries

If you're arriving from nearby countries like New Zealand, Indonesia, or Singapore, here's how to reach Australia by rail:

1. Fly Into Major Cities: Arrive via international airports in Sydney, Melbourne, Brisbane, Perth, or Darwin.
2. Transfer to Train Stations: Most cities have direct links between airports and central train stations via shuttle buses, taxis, or public transport.
3. Pre-Book Domestic Connections: If needed, arrange domestic flights or buses to reach departure points for routes like The Ghan or Indian Pacific.

Consider purchasing an open-jaw ticket (flying into one city and out of another) to maximize convenience.

## 4.10 Seven-Day Sample Itinerary

Here's an example of a weeklong rail journey combining multiple iconic routes:

- Day 1: Arrive in Sydney and board the Indian Pacific. Enjoy dinner as you depart for Broken Hill.
- Day 2–3: Cross the Nullarbor Plain; enjoy stargazing and optional tours in Kalgoorlie.
- Day 4: Arrive in Perth. Spend the day exploring Kings Park and Fremantle.
- Day 5: Fly to Adelaide and board the Overland to Melbourne. Stop en route for wine tastings.
- Day 6: Explore Melbourne's laneways and take a day trip to the Great Ocean Road.
- Day 7: Depart for home or extend your stay to explore Tasmania or Queensland.

## Chapter 5: Life on the Rails

Traveling by train in Australia is more than just a means of getting from one place to another—it's an immersive experience. From sleeping arrangements and gourmet meals to onboard entertainment and adapting to time zones, this chapter will guide you through what life on the rails feels like. Whether you're in a luxury cabin or an economy seat, we'll help you make the most of your journey.

## 5.1 What to Expect During Your Journey

Life on the rails offers a unique blend of relaxation, adventure, and discovery. Here's what you can expect during your Australian rail journey:

- Scenic Views: Trains traverse some of the most stunning landscapes in the world—from the red sands of the Outback to lush rainforests and rugged coastlines. Large panoramic windows ensure unobstructed views.

- **Rhythmic Motion:** The gentle sway of the train creates a soothing environment, perfect for unwinding after a busy day of sightseeing or simply enjoying the ride.

- **Friendly Atmosphere:** Fellow passengers are often eager to share stories, tips, and laughter. Strike up conversations over meals or in communal lounges.

- **Off-Train Excursions:** Many routes include stops where you can disembark for guided tours, hikes, or cultural experiences before reboarding.

- **Onboard Staff:** Attentive crew members are available to assist with everything from luggage handling to answering questions about the route.

Whether you're chasing solitude or social interaction, train travel caters to all preferences.

## 5.2 Sleeping Comfortably in Cabins or Seats

A good night's sleep is essential for making the most of your journey. Here's how to rest comfortably depending on your accommodation class:

- Platinum Service (Luxury Cabins):
- Private cabins feature double beds, ensuite bathrooms, and climate control.
- Beds are made up freshly each evening by attentive stewards.
- Noise-canceling features ensure a peaceful night's rest despite the train's motion.

- Gold Service (Sleeper Berths):
- Compact but cozy berths convert into comfortable beds at night.
- Shared restroom facilities are clean and well-maintained.
- Curtains provide privacy, and earplugs/eye masks may be provided upon request.

- Economy Class (Reclining Seats):
- While not ideal for long overnight legs, reclining seats offer basic comfort for shorter trips.
- Bring a neck pillow, blanket, and eye mask for added coziness.
- If traveling Economy overnight, consider breaking up the journey with stopovers in towns along the way.

**Pro Tip: Pack lightweight pajamas and slippers to enhance your comfort during overnight journeys.**

## 5.3 Dining Cars and Meals on Board

Dining onboard Australian trains is an experience in itself. Here's what to expect:

- Included Meals: Most Gold and Platinum services offer breakfast, lunch, dinner, and snacks as part of your fare. Menus highlight regional ingredients and flavors:
- Breakfast: Fresh fruit, yogurt, cereals, eggs, bacon, and pastries.
- Lunch/Dinner: Multi-course meals featuring dishes like barramundi, kangaroo fillet, and grilled vegetables. Vegetarian, vegan, and gluten-free options are usually available upon request.

- Beverages: Complimentary tea, coffee, soft drinks, beer, and wine are often included. Some trains even host onboard wine tastings showcasing local vineyards.

- Dining Cars: Meals are served in elegant dining cars with panoramic windows, allowing you to enjoy both food and scenery simultaneously.

- Economy Class: For budget travelers, bring your own snacks or purchase affordable meals from onboard kiosks.

Make sure to notify operators of any dietary restrictions when booking so they can accommodate your needs.

## 5.4 Entertainment and Activities While Traveling

Train journeys are filled with opportunities to relax, explore, and engage. Here's what keeps passengers entertained:

- Panoramic Windows: Spend hours gazing at ever-changing landscapes—whether it's the golden hues of the Nullarbor Plain or the tropical greenery of Queensland.

- Guided Tours and Talks: Many trains offer onboard presentations about Indigenous culture, history, and geography. Some excursions also include nature walks or wildlife spotting.

- Social Spaces: Lounges and observation decks encourage mingling with fellow travelers. Share stories, play board games, or sip cocktails while watching the sunset.

- Photography Opportunities: Capture iconic moments like sunrise over the desert or reflections on waterways. Early mornings and late afternoons are prime times for photography.

- Special Events: Seasonal trains sometimes host themed events, such as Christmas dinners or stargazing nights under the Milky Way.

Embrace the slower pace of train travel—it's part of the charm!

## 5.5 Tips for Staying Entertained: Books, Podcasts, Games, and More

Long train rides provide ample time to indulge in hobbies or discover new interests. Here are some ideas to keep you entertained:

- Books: Bring novels, travel guides, or memoirs set in Australia. E-readers are convenient for carrying multiple titles without extra weight.

- Podcasts/Audiobooks: Listen to true crime, comedy, or educational podcasts about Australian history and wildlife. Audiobooks are great companions for scenic stretches.

- Games: Pack compact items like playing cards, travel-sized chess sets, or puzzles. Solo games like Sudoku or crossword books work well too.

- Music and Movies: Create playlists of relaxing tunes or download movies/TV shows to watch offline.

- Journaling: Document your journey by writing reflections, sketching landscapes, or jotting down memorable moments.

- People-Watching: Observe fellow passengers and strike up conversations—you never know who you might meet!

Staying entertained is easy when you come prepared with activities that suit your personality.

## 5.6 Navigating Time Zones and Long Distances

Australia spans three main time zones, which can be confusing for first-time visitors. Here's how to navigate them seamlessly:

- Eastern Standard Time (EST): Covers Sydney, Melbourne, Brisbane, and Canberra.
- Central Standard Time (CST): Applies to Adelaide and Darwin (30 minutes behind EST).
- Western Standard Time (WST): Used in Perth (2 hours behind CST).

Tips for Managing Time Zones:
- Adjust your watch whenever crossing into a new zone. Most trains display current times onboard.
- Use apps like World Clock to stay organized if connecting flights or meetings are involved.
- Take advantage of longer days during daylight saving periods (October–April in some states).

Adapting to Long Distances:
- Break up your trip with stopovers in interesting towns along the route.
- Stay hydrated and stretch regularly to combat fatigue.
- Embrace the rhythm of the rails—long distances mean more time to relax and soak in the scenery.

**By staying mindful of time zones and pacing yourself, you'll glide effortlessly across the vast Australian landscape.**

## Chapter 6: Culinary Delights Along the Rails

One of the greatest pleasures of traveling by train in Australia is indulging in its culinary offerings. From gourmet meals prepared with fresh, local ingredients to casual eats inspired by regional flavors, Australian rail journeys are a feast for the senses. In this chapter, we'll explore the delicious dishes served onboard and highlight must-try foods at major stops along the way.

### 6.1 Savoring Regional Cuisine Onboard

Australian trains take pride in showcasing regional cuisine, offering passengers a taste of the destinations they're passing through. Each route features menus crafted to reflect the unique landscapes, cultures, and produce of the areas they traverse. Whether you're sipping Barossa Valley wine or sampling barramundi caught fresh from tropical waters, dining onboard is an integral part of the journey.

Pro Tip: Notify operators of any dietary restrictions when booking so they can tailor meals to your needs.

## 6.2 Highlights from The Ghan's Outback Dinners

The Ghan is renowned not just for its stunning scenery but also for its exceptional dining experiences. Meals aboard this legendary train celebrate the rugged beauty of the Outback with hearty, flavorful dishes:

- Breakfast: Start your day with classics like scrambled eggs, bacon, and grilled tomatoes, alongside native ingredients such as wattleseed pancakes.
- Lunch/Dinner: Feast on slow-cooked lamb shoulder, kangaroo fillet, or crocodile sliders paired with seasonal vegetables.
- Desserts: Indulge in treats like quandong tart (made from native peach) or chocolate mousse infused with bush spices.

Each meal tells a story of the land, blending modern techniques with traditional flavors.

## 6.3 Fine Dining on Indian Pacific: Multi-Course Menus with Local Ingredients

The Indian Pacific elevates rail dining to an art form, serving multi-course meals that rival those of high-end restaurants. Passengers enjoy dishes made with premium ingredients sourced from across Australia:

- Appetizers: Try smoked salmon cured in Margaret River olive oil or marinated prawns with lemon myrtle aioli.
- Mains: Options range from grass-fed beef tenderloin to Tasmanian salmon accompanied by truffle mashed potatoes.
- Cheese Platters: Sample artisanal cheeses from South Australia's dairy regions.
- Wine Pairings: Enjoy award-winning wines from Clare Valley, Coonawarra, and beyond.

The elegant dining car provides panoramic views, making every bite feel like a celebration of Australia's bounty.

## 6.4 Casual Eats on Spirit of Queensland: Fresh Seafood and Tropics-Inspired Dishes

For a more laid-back vibe, the Spirit of Queensland offers casual yet satisfying meals inspired by tropical North Queensland:

- Seafood Staples: Barramundi tacos, Moreton Bay bug rolls, and chilled prawn cocktails showcase the region's oceanic riches.
- Tropical Flavors: Dishes often incorporate mango salsa, macadamia nuts, and lime-infused dressings for a refreshing twist.
- Snacks: Grab a quick bite like banana bread or coconut lamingtons while gazing at lush rainforests outside your window.

Even Economy passengers can purchase affordable meals featuring these vibrant flavors.

## 6.5 Must-Try Foods at Major Stops

Train travel allows you to disembark at fascinating destinations where local delicacies await. Here are some must-try foods at key stops along Australia's iconic routes:

- Alice Springs (The Ghan): Bush tucker-inspired dishes like camel burgers and damper bread.

-Katherine (The Ghan): Freshwater fish caught from nearby rivers, often served grilled or in curries.
- Broken Hill (Indian Pacific): Silver City sausages and locally brewed craft beers.
-Barossa Valley (Indian Pacific): World-famous Shiraz wines and handmade chocolates.
- Cairns (Spirit of Queensland): Tropical fruits like papaya, lychee, and finger limes straight from the source.

These stops provide opportunities to immerse yourself in regional food culture.

## 6.6 Oysters in Coffin Bay (The Ghan)

No visit to Coffin Bay—a picturesque bay near Port Lincoln—is complete without sampling its world-class oysters. These briny beauties are known for their creamy texture and subtle sweetness, thanks to the pristine waters they're harvested from. Many excursions include oyster tastings paired with sparkling wine, creating a luxurious seaside experience.

**Fun Fact:** Coffin Bay oysters are sustainably farmed, ensuring minimal environmental impact.

## 6.7 Barossa Valley Wines (Indian Pacific)

The Barossa Valley is synonymous with fine wine, particularly bold reds like Shiraz and Cabernet Sauvignon. Passengers on the Indian Pacific often have the chance to tour this iconic wine region during off-train excursions. Highlights include:

- Wine Tastings: Visit cellar doors at legendary estates like Penfolds, Jacob's Creek, and Seppeltsfield.
- Food Pairings: Savor platters of cured meats, olives, and artisanal cheeses alongside your favorite vintages.
- Exclusive Bottlings: Purchase limited-edition bottles only available directly from the vineyards.

Even if you don't leave the train, many meals onboard feature Barossa Valley wines, allowing you to savor the region's essence without stepping off.

## 6.8 Tropical Fruits in Cairns (Spirit of Queensland)

Cairns is a paradise for fruit lovers, offering access to some of Australia's most exotic produce. During your stop here, make time to visit local markets or orchards to try:

- Mangosteens: Sweet and tangy with a soft, juicy interior.
- Rambutans: Fuzzy red fruits bursting with fragrant, floral flavor.
- Finger Limes: Tiny citrus pods filled with caviar-like juice bursts.

Many cafes and restaurants in Cairns incorporate these fruits into smoothie bowls, desserts, and cocktails—perfect for cooling off in the tropical heat.

## 6.9 Special Dietary Needs: Vegan, Vegetarian, and Gluten-Free Options

Australia's rail operators cater to multiple dietary requirements, ensuring everyone enjoys their meals. Here's how they accommodate special needs:

- Vegan Options: Plant-based dishes like roasted vegetable risottos, lentil stews, and dairy-free desserts are readily available.
- Vegetarian Choices: Expect creative vegetarian mains like eggplant parmigiana, mushroom pasta, and stuffed capsicums.

- Gluten-Free Alternatives: Most operators stock gluten-free bread, pasta, and baked goods upon request.

When booking, specify your dietary preferences so chefs can prepare suitable meals ahead of time. Don't hesitate to ask staff for recommendations—they're happy to help!

**Final Thoughts**

From lavish onboard dinners to mouthwatering street food at stops along the way, Australia's rail journeys offer endless opportunities to indulge in culinary delights. Whether you're savoring native ingredients, sampling world-class wines, or exploring tropical fruit markets, each bite adds another layer to your adventure.

## Chapter 7: Accommodations Options Near Train Stations

After disembarking from your train journey, finding the right place to stay can enhance your overall travel experience. Whether you're seeking luxury hotels, quirky boutique stays, or budget-friendly hostels, Australia offers a wide range of accommodation options near major train stations and along popular routes. In this chapter, we'll guide you through the best lodging choices to suit every traveler's style and budget.

### 7.1 Luxury Hotels Close to Major Stations

For travelers who value comfort, elegance, and convenience, luxury hotels near train stations provide the perfect base for exploring cities or preparing for your next leg of the journey:

- Sydney: The Langham Sydney and Park Hyatt Sydney are both within walking distance of Central

Station and Circular Quay, offering stunning views of the harbor and opulent amenities.
- Melbourne: Crown Towers Melbourne, located near Southern Cross Station, boasts lavish rooms, fine dining restaurants, and a world-class spa.
- Perth: COMO The Treasury, situated in the heart of Perth near Perth Station, combines historic charm with modern luxury, featuring rooftop pools and exquisite architecture.
- Adelaide: Mayfair Hotel Adelaide, close to Adelaide Railway Station, offers boutique luxury with beautifully designed interiors and exceptional service.

These hotels often include perks like concierge services, room upgrades, and exclusive access to local attractions.

## 7.2 Boutique Stays in Sydney, Melbourne, and Perth

Boutique accommodations blend character, style, and personalized service, making them ideal for travelers seeking unique experiences:

- Sydney: Ovolo Woolloomooloo is a chic waterfront hotel housed in a heritage-listed building, just minutes

from Kings Cross Station. Its vibrant design and complimentary happy hour make it a favorite among visitors.
- Melbourne: Coppersmith Hotel in South Melbourne (near Flinders Street Station) exudes industrial charm with its exposed brick walls, cozy lounges, and farm-to-table restaurant.
- Perth: Alex Hotel in Northbridge offers minimalist Scandinavian-inspired rooms and a relaxed rooftop bar, perfect for unwinding after a day of exploration.

Boutique stays are great for those who want a more intimate and memorable experience compared to large chain hotels.

## 7.3 Desert Resorts in Alice Springs and Darwin

If you're venturing into Australia's arid interior or tropical north, desert resorts offer a serene escape amidst breathtaking landscapes:

Alice Springs:
- L'Auberge de L'Outback: A charming resort with spacious suites, lush gardens, and an outdoor pool,

located just a short drive from Alice Springs Railway Station.
- **Sails in the Desert Hotel:** Part of the Ayers Rock Resort complex near Uluru, this property features Aboriginal art galleries, cultural performances, and luxurious rooms overlooking the Outback.

Darwin:
- **Hilton Darwin:** Overlooking the waterfront, this upscale hotel is conveniently close to Darwin Railway Station and offers panoramic city views, infinity pools, and easy access to Mindil Beach Markets.
- **Vibe Hotel Darwin Waterfront:** Modern and stylish, this hotel places you steps away from Crocosaurus Cove and the scenic Esplanade.

Desert resorts combine relaxation with opportunities to immerse yourself in the rugged beauty of regional Australia.

## 7.4 Budget-Friendly Hostels and Guesthouses

For backpackers, solo travelers, and families on a tight budget, hostels and guesthouses provide affordable yet comfortable lodging:

- **Hostels:** Chains like YHA Australia and Mad Monkey Hostels operate clean, social spaces near train stations in cities like Brisbane, Melbourne, and Cairns. Many offer private rooms as well as dormitory-style accommodations.
- **Guesthouses:** Family-run guesthouses in smaller towns like Katherine and Broken Hill provide homey vibes with shared kitchens, communal areas, and warm hospitality.
- **Budget Chains:** Brands like Ibis Budget and Quest Apartments cater to cost-conscious travelers without sacrificing basic comforts.

While these options may lack frills, they're excellent for meeting fellow travelers and stretching your travel budget further.

## 7.5 Unique Lodging Experiences

Why settle for ordinary when you can sleep somewhere extraordinary? Australia is full of quirky and unforgettable lodging options:

-**Treehouses:** Stay in treehouse accommodations like TreeTops Rainforest Lodge in Queensland's Daintree Rainforest for a magical jungle retreat.

- Converted Trains: Old railway carriages have been transformed into unique lodgings, such as the Train Carriage Apartments in Victoria's Daylesford region.
- Underground Bunkers: Experience life underground at the Desert Cave Hotel in Coober Pedy, where rooms are carved into the earth to escape the heat.

Unique stays add an element of adventure to your trip and create lifelong memories.

## 7.6 Glamping Under the Stars Near Uluru

Glamping (glamorous camping) combines the thrill of sleeping outdoors with the luxuries of a hotel. Near Uluru, several glamping sites allow you to connect with nature while enjoying top-notch amenities:

- Longitude 131°: This ultra-luxurious eco-resort offers tented pavilions with floor-to-ceiling windows facing Uluru. Enjoy guided tours, gourmet meals, and stargazing sessions under the vast Outback sky.
- Kings Canyon Resort Glamping: Located between Uluru and Alice Springs, this site provides safari-style tents with plush beds, en-suite bathrooms, and private decks overlooking the desert.

Glamping lets you embrace the wilderness without compromising on comfort—a must-do for any Outback adventure.

## 7.7 Heritage Cottages in Historic Towns Like Broken Hill

Australia's historic towns are rich in character, and staying in a heritage cottage allows you to step back in time:

- Broken Hill: Book a stay at one of the town's restored miners' cottages, complete with vintage furnishings and period details. Properties like The Lodge Outback Retreat blend history with modern conveniences.
- Port Fairy: On Victoria's Great Ocean Road, charming cottages like Drift House offer ocean views and elegant interiors inspired by the town's maritime past.

Heritage cottages are perfect for travelers who appreciate storytelling through architecture and decor.

## 7.8 Tips for Booking Last-Minute Stays During Peak Seasons

Peak seasons—such as school holidays, Christmas, and major events—can make finding accommodations challenging. Here are some tips to secure last-minute stays:

- Use Booking Apps: Platforms like Booking.com, Expedia, and Airbnb allow you to filter available properties instantly.
- Check Local Tourism Websites: Regional tourism boards often list lesser-known hotels, motels, and bed-and-breakfasts that might not appear on larger booking sites.
- Contact Directly: Reach out to hotels directly via phone or email; sometimes they hold unsold rooms until the last minute.
- Be Flexible: Consider staying slightly outside the city center or opting for alternative accommodations like vacation rentals or campsites.
- Join Loyalty Programs: Membership in hotel loyalty programs can give you priority access to limited inventory during busy periods.

**Pro Tip:** Always carry a backup plan, such as emergency contacts for hostels or budget chains, in case preferred options fall through.

**Final Thoughts**

**Whether you choose to indulge in five-star luxury, embrace quirky boutiques, or rough it in a hostel dorm, there's no shortage of incredible places to stay near Australia's train stations. Your choice of accommodation can shape your entire journey, so take the time to find something that aligns with your preferences and budget.**

## Chapter 8: Transportation Beyond Trains

While trains are an incredible way to traverse Australia, your journey doesn't have to end when you disembark. Exploring cities, regional areas, and remote destinations often requires additional modes of transportation. In this chapter, we'll guide you through navigating beyond the rails, from public transit systems and car rentals to guided tours and eco-friendly options like cycling and walking trails.

## 8.1 Navigating Cities and Regions After Disembarking

Once you step off the train, you'll need reliable ways to reach your next destination—whether it's a hotel, attraction, or another mode of transport. Here's how to navigate efficiently:

- Plan Ahead: Research transportation options for your arrival city before your trip. Many train stations have information desks, maps, and signage to help orient you.

- Use Apps: Navigation apps like Google Maps, Moovit, or local transit-specific apps can provide real-time updates on buses, trams, and shuttles.
- Ask Locals: Station staff, taxi drivers, or fellow travelers are excellent resources for tips on getting around.

Pro Tip: Keep spare cash handy for taxis or rideshare services if public transport isn't immediately available.

## 8.2 Public Transit Systems in Major Cities

Australia's major cities boast efficient and user-friendly public transit networks that connect train stations with key attractions and neighborhoods:

Sydney:
- Use the Opal Card for seamless access to trains, buses, ferries, and light rail. Highlights include the free City Circle tram and scenic ferry rides across Sydney Harbour.

Melbourne:

- The Myki card grants access to trams, trains, and buses. Don't miss the free City Loop tram zone and Melbourne's iconic cable car network.

Brisbane:
- The Go Card works across buses, trains, and ferries. Take a Rivercat ferry along the Brisbane River for stunning skyline views.

Perth:
- Perth's SmartRider card covers trains, buses, and free CAT (Central Area Transit) buses within the CBD. Explore Kings Park or cycle along the Swan River using bike paths.

- Adelaide:
- Adelaide's MetroCARD simplifies travel on trains, trams, and buses. Enjoy the free City Connector bus loop to explore North Adelaide and the city center.

Public transit is affordable, convenient, and eco-friendly—a great way to plunge into urban life.

## 8.3 Renting Cars for Road Trips Around Regional Areas

If you're eager to explore beyond cities, renting a car opens up endless possibilities for road trips through Australia's multiple landscapes. Here's what to know:

- Where to Rent: Companies like Avis, Hertz, and Budget operate at major train stations and airports. Compare prices online to find the best deals.
- Types of Vehicles: Choose compact cars for solo travelers or small groups, SUVs for rugged terrain, or campervans for a self-contained adventure.
- Must-Know Rules: Familiarize yourself with Australian driving laws, including speed limits, seatbelt requirements, and wildlife awareness (especially at dawn and dusk).
- Popular Routes:
- The Great Ocean Road (Victoria): Drive past Twelve Apostles and coastal cliffs after disembarking in Melbourne.
- Red Centre Way (Northern Territory): Explore Uluru, Kings Canyon, and Alice Springs after riding The Ghan.
- Margaret River Region (Western Australia): Visit wineries, beaches, and caves near Perth following your Indian Pacific journey.

Renting a car gives you freedom and flexibility to create your own itinerary.

## 8.4 Guided Tours and Shuttles for Day Excursions

For travelers who prefer hassle-free adventures, guided tours and shuttle services are fantastic options:

- Guided Tours: Join organized day trips to iconic landmarks like Kakadu National Park (from Darwin), the Blue Mountains (from Sydney), or Phillip Island (from Melbourne). These tours often include meals, entry fees, and knowledgeable guides.
- Shuttle Services: Many regional towns offer shared shuttles to nearby attractions. For example:
- Nitmiluk Tours runs shuttles from Katherine to Katherine Gorge for river cruises and hikes.
- Cairns-based shuttles take passengers to the Daintree Rainforest or Great Barrier Reef.

Guided tours and shuttles are ideal for those short on time or unfamiliar with the area.

## 8.5 Connecting Flights for International Travelers

If you're visiting Australia as part of a larger international itinerary, connecting flights may be necessary to continue your journey:

- Domestic Airlines: Qantas, Virgin Australia, Jetstar, and Rex operate domestic routes linking major cities and regional hubs. Book early to secure competitive fares.
- Airport Transfers: Most train stations in capital cities offer direct connections to airports via dedicated trains, buses, or taxis. Examples include:
- Sydney Airport Link Train from Central Station.
- SkyBus from Southern Cross Station to Melbourne Airport.
- Perth Airport Shuttle from Perth Station.

Coordinate flight times carefully to allow ample buffer between train arrivals and departures.

## 8.6 Cycling and Walking Trails for Eco-Conscious Adventurers

For environmentally conscious travelers, cycling and walking trails provide sustainable ways to explore Australia's natural beauty and cultural heritage:

- Cycling Trails:
- Murray to Mountains Rail Trail (Victoria): Pedal through picturesque farmland and historic towns after alighting in Albury/Wodonga.
-Bikeway Network (Brisbane): Follow riverside paths and green corridors to discover hidden gems in the city.
- Rottnest Island (Western Australia): Rent a bike to cruise around this car-free paradise.

- Walking Trails:
- Bondi to Coogee Coastal Walk (Sydney): Enjoy ocean vistas and secluded beaches after arriving at Circular Quay.
-Larapinta Trail (Northern Territory): Commence on multi-day hikes through the West MacDonnell Ranges near Alice Springs.
- Fremantle Heritage Trail (Perth): Stroll through historic streets lined with colonial architecture.

Cycling and walking are low-impact ways to immerse yourself in Australia's landscapes while reducing your carbon footprint.

Final Thoughts

Transportation beyond trains ensures you can fully experience all that Australia has to offer—from bustling metropolises to serene Outback retreats. Whether you opt for public transit, rent a car, join a guided tour, or embrace eco-friendly alternatives, each mode of transport adds a new dimension to your journey.

## Chapter 9: Exploring Major Cities in Australia by Rail

Australia's major cities are vibrant hubs of culture, history, and natural beauty, each offering a unique experience. Thanks to the country's extensive rail network, you can easily access these urban centers and explore their highlights using convenient public transportation systems. In this chapter, we'll guide you through eight iconic Australian cities, showcasing must-see attractions and how to navigate them seamlessly after arriving by train.

## 9.1 Sydney: Coastal Charm and Urban Energy

Sydney is a dazzling blend of cosmopolitan sophistication and laid-back coastal charm. From its world-famous landmarks to pristine beaches, there's something for everyone in this dynamic city.

**Highlights:**

- **Opera House:** A UNESCO World Heritage Site and architectural masterpiece—attend a performance or take a guided tour.
- **Harbour Bridge:** Walk across or climb to the top for panoramic views of the harbor.
- **Bondi Beach:** Surf, swim, or stroll along one of Australia's most iconic stretches of sand.

Getting Around:
- **Trams:** The light rail connects key areas like Central Station, Darling Harbour, and Circular Quay.
- **Ferries:** Hop on a ferry at Circular Quay to explore destinations like Manly, Taronga Zoo, and Watsons Bay.
- **Suburban Trains:** Use the CityRail network to venture further afield, such as to the Blue Mountains or Northern Beaches.

Pro Tip: Don't miss the free City Circle tram, which loops around major attractions in the CBD.

## 9.2 Melbourne: Culture, Cafés, and Hidden Laneways

Melbourne is known for its artsy vibe, café culture, and hidden treasures tucked away in narrow laneways. This creative capital is perfect for foodies, shoppers, and adventurers alike.

Highlights:
- Federation Square: A bustling hub of galleries, restaurants, and events overlooking the Yarra River.
- Yarra River: Take a riverside walk or kayak down the waterway for a different perspective of the city.
- Great Ocean Road: While not directly in Melbourne, this scenic drive (accessible via regional trains) leads to dramatic cliffs and surf spots.

Getting Around:
- City Circle Tram: Free rides loop through the heart of Melbourne, connecting landmarks like Queen Victoria Market and Docklands.
- Metro System: Melbourne's train network makes it easy to reach suburbs like St Kilda, Brunswick, and Brighton Beach.

Fun Fact: Melbourne is often called the "coffee capital" of Australia—be sure to try a flat white!

## 9.3 Brisbane: Gateway to Sunshine and Surf

Brisbane combines subtropical warmth with modern amenities, making it an inviting base for exploring Queensland's sun-soaked coastlines and wildlife-rich hinterlands.

Highlights:
- South Bank: Enjoy man-made beaches, art galleries, and riverside dining.
- Lone Pine Koala Sanctuary: Get up close with native animals like kangaroos and koalas.
- Gold Coast: Just a short train ride south, this glitzy destination boasts theme parks, surfing, and nightlife.

Getting Around:
- RiverCat Ferries: Cruise along the Brisbane River to discover waterfront neighborhoods like New Farm and Kangaroo Point.
- CityLoop Trains: These underground loops connect major stations and attractions within the CBD.

Pro Tip: Rent a bike to cycle along the Brisbane Riverwalk for stunning skyline views.

## 9.4 Adelaide: Wine Country and Festivals Galore

Adelaide exudes charm with its historic architecture, thriving arts scene, and proximity to some of Australia's finest wine regions. It's also known as the "festival city" due to its year-round celebrations.

Highlights:
- Barossa Valley: Sample world-class Shiraz wines just an hour's train ride away.
- Adelaide Hills: Explore quaint villages, Mount Lofty Summit, and Cleland Wildlife Park.
- Central Market: Indulge in gourmet produce, cheeses, and multicultural street food.

Getting Around:
- Free City Connector Buses: Circulate through the CBD and North Adelaide, stopping near popular sights.
- Trains: Regional services link Adelaide to nearby towns and vineyards, including Barossa Valley and McLaren Vale.

Fun Fact: Adelaide hosts the annual WOMADelaide music festival—a must-visit for global music fans.

## 9.5 Perth: Modern Meets Natural Beauty

Perth balances urban sophistication with easy access to nature, from sprawling parks to pristine islands. Its relaxed pace and sunny weather make it a favorite among travelers.

Highlights:
- **Kings Park:** One of the largest inner-city parks in the world, featuring native flora and sweeping city views.
- **Rottnest Island:** Catch a ferry from Fremantle to meet quokkas and enjoy snorkeling or biking.
- **Swan Valley Wineries:** Sip local wines and ciders in this picturesque region just outside the city.

Getting Around:
- **Perth Train Network:** Connects the CBD with suburbs like Fremantle, Cottesloe Beach, and Swan Valley.
- **Bicycles:** Perth is bike-friendly, with dedicated paths along the Swan River and throughout the city.

Pro Tip: Visit Elizabeth Quay for cafes, playgrounds, and paddleboarding opportunities.

## 9.6 Cairns: Tropical Paradise and Reef Adventures

Cairns serves as the gateway to two UNESCO World Heritage Sites—the Great Barrier Reef and the Daintree Rainforest. This tropical haven is perfect for adventure seekers and nature lovers.

**Highlights:**
- Great Barrier Reef: Snorkel, Plunge, or take a glass-bottom boat tour to marvel at coral reefs and marine life.
- Daintree Rainforest: Discover ancient rainforests, crocodile-spotting cruises, and Mossman Gorge.
- Esplanade Lagoon: Swim in the artificial lagoon or relax on the grassy lawns overlooking Trinity Inlet.

**Getting Around:**
- Skyrail Rainforest Cableway: Glide above the rainforest canopy between Cairns and Kuranda.
- Local Buses: Sunbus operates routes throughout Cairns and surrounding areas, including Palm Cove and Port Douglas.

**Pro Tip:** Join a day trip to Cape Tribulation for a true rainforest-meets-beach experience.

## 9.7 Darwin: Outback Vibes and Indigenous Culture

**Darwin offers a mix of rugged Outback charm and rich Indigenous heritage. As Australia's northernmost capital, it's your starting point for exploring national parks and remote wilderness.**

**Highlights:**
**- Mindil Beach Markets: Shop for local crafts, enjoy sunset dinners, and watch fireworks over the Timor Sea.**
**- Kakadu National Park: Accessible via organized tours, this park features wetlands, rock art, and multiple wildlife.**

**Getting Around:**
**- Shuttle Services: Many hotels and attractions offer shuttle transfers from Darwin Railway Station.**
**- Self-Drive Options: Renting a car gives you flexibility to visit Litchfield National Park or venture into Kakadu.**

**Fun Fact: Darwin's dry season (May–October) is festival season, with events like the Darwin Festival and Deckchair Cinema.**

## 9.8 Alice Springs: Heart of the Red Centre

Alice Springs lies at the heart of Australia's Red Centre, surrounded by desert landscapes and sacred Aboriginal sites. It's the ideal base for exploring iconic Outback destinations.

Highlights:
- Uluru: Witness sunrise or sunset over this monolithic rock formation steeped in spiritual significance.
- MacDonnell Ranges: Hike through gorges, swim in waterholes, and admire ochre-colored cliffs.
-Aboriginal Art Centers: Learn about Indigenous culture and purchase authentic artworks.

Getting Around:
- Car Rentals: Essential for reaching Uluru, Kings Canyon, and other remote locations.
- Guided Tours: Join small-group excursions to maximize your time and knowledge of the area.

Pro Tip: Visit the Royal Flying Doctor Service Museum to learn about healthcare in remote Australia.

Final Thoughts

Exploring Australia's major cities by rail opens doors to unforgettable experiences—from Sydney's sparkling harbors to Alice Springs' mystical deserts. Each city has its own personality, but they all share one thing in common: accessibility via Australia's efficient rail system. Combine train travel with local transport options to uncover hidden gems and create memories that last a lifetime.

## Chapter 10: Scenic Highlights Along the Way

One of the greatest joys of traveling by train in Australia is the ever-changing scenery outside your window. From the fiery red deserts of Central Australia to the lush rainforests of Tropical Queensland, every route offers breathtaking landscapes that unfold like a living painting. In this chapter, we'll highlight some of the most iconic and awe-inspiring sights you'll encounter during your rail journey—and how to make the most of them.

## 10.1 Must-See Landscapes from Your Window

Australia's railways traverse some of the most diverse and dramatic terrains on Earth. Keep your camera ready, because these are the moments you won't want to miss:

- Golden Sunrises: Watch as dawn paints the horizon in hues of orange, pink, and purple, illuminating vast plains or rugged mountains.

- **Star-Filled Nights:** On clear evenings, gaze out at the Milky Way stretching across the sky—a sight especially magical in remote areas like the Nullarbor Plain.
- **Seasonal Changes:** Depending on when you travel, you might see wildflowers blooming in spring, snow-capped peaks in winter, or vibrant greenery after summer rains.

Pro Tip: Sit on the side of the train facing the direction of travel for uninterrupted views (and fewer shadows on your photos).

## 10.2 Red Deserts of Central Australia

The Outback is synonymous with Australia's identity, and no rail journey captures its essence better than The Ghan. As you glide through Central Australia, prepare to be mesmerized by:

- **Endless Red Sands:** The arid yet strikingly beautiful desert stretches as far as the eye can see, dotted with sparse vegetation and ancient gum trees.
- **MacDonnell Ranges:** Jagged ridges rise dramatically against the skyline, hinting at millions of years of geological history.

- **Uluru (Ayers Rock):** Even if you don't disembark, catching a glimpse of this iconic monolith from afar is unforgettable—it glows brilliantly during sunrise and sunset.

**Fun Fact:** The Outback covers over 70% of Australia's landmass but is home to less than 10% of its population, making it one of the world's last true wildernesses.

## 10.3 Lush Rainforests of Tropical Queensland

The Spirit of Queensland takes you through some of Australia's wettest and most biodiverse regions. Look out for:

- **Daintree Rainforest:** This ancient ecosystem predates the Amazon by millions of years and teems with life—watch for flashes of iridescent butterflies and towering ferns.
- **Tropical Coastlines:** Pristine beaches meet dense jungle, creating a stunning contrast between turquoise waters and emerald foliage.
- **Sugar Cane Fields:** Rolling fields of sugar cane line parts of the route, offering insight into Queensland's agricultural heritage.

Photography Tip: Use polarized lenses to reduce glare when shooting reflections off rivers and lagoons.

## 10.4 Vast Plains of the Nullarbor

The Indian Pacific crosses one of the planet's largest expanses of flat, treeless land—the Nullarbor Plain. While seemingly barren, this region holds an austere beauty:

- Infinite Horizons: The sheer scale of the plain makes it feel otherworldly, with nothing interrupting the view except occasional salt lakes or limestone cliffs.
- Nullarbor Roadhouse: A quirky stop where travelers can stretch their legs and learn about life in this isolated corner of Australia.
- Stargazing Opportunities: With minimal light pollution, the Nullarbor offers unparalleled night skies filled with constellations and shooting stars.

Insider Tip: Bring binoculars for daytime spotting of wedge-tailed eagles soaring overhead.

## 10.5 Wildlife Spotting Opportunities

Australian trains pass through habitats rich in native wildlife. Keep your eyes peeled for these incredible creatures:

- Kangaroos and Wallabies: Often spotted bounding alongside tracks in rural and Outback areas.
- Emus and Wedge-Tailed Eagles: These majestic birds are frequently seen near open grasslands and plains.
- Camels and Brumbies: Wild camels roam freely in Central Australia, while brumby horses gallop across alpine regions.
- Marine Life: Coastal routes may reveal dolphins, sea turtles, and even migrating whales during certain seasons.

Wildlife Watching Tip: Early mornings and late afternoons are prime times for animal activity.

## 10.6 Sunrise and Sunset Moments Over Iconic Terrain

Few experiences rival witnessing sunrise or sunset from the comfort of a train carriage. Here's why these moments are so special:

- **The Ghan:** As the sun rises over the Outback, the red sands glow with an ethereal intensity, while sunsets bathe Uluru in fiery tones.
- **Indian Pacific:** Watch the golden light dance across the Nullarbor Plain or illuminate the Blue Mountains' misty valleys.
- **Spirit of Queensland:** Tropical sunrises cast shimmering reflections on calm seas, while sunsets paint the rainforest canopy in deep oranges and purples.

**Photography Tip:** Set your camera to "sunset mode" or adjust exposure manually to capture vivid colors without losing detail.

**Final Thoughts**

The scenic highlights along Australia's rail routes are nothing short of extraordinary. Each moment—from the stark beauty of the Outback to the verdant splendor of rainforests—offers a chance to connect with nature and reflect on the vastness of this incredible continent.

## Chapter 11: Off-Train Adventures

Australia's iconic train journeys aren't just about the ride—they're gateways to unforgettable off-train adventures. From exploring ancient landscapes and vibrant ecosystems to indulging in regional cuisines and cultural experiences, stopovers and excursions add depth and excitement to your rail journey. In this chapter, we'll guide you through making the most of your time off the train, highlighting must-see destinations and offering tips for crafting your perfect detour.

## 11.1 Making the Most of Stopovers and Excursions

Stopovers are a golden opportunity to stretch your legs, immerse yourself in local culture, and discover hidden gems along your route. Here's how to maximize these moments:

- **Plan Ahead:** Research optional excursions offered by train operators or book independently based on your interests.
- **Pack Smart:** Bring essentials like sunscreen, water bottles, hats, and comfortable walking shoes for outdoor activities.
- **Stay Flexible:** While it's tempting to stick to a tight schedule, leave room for spontaneity—sometimes the best memories come from unplanned discoveries.
- **Capture Memories:** Take photos, jot down notes, or collect small mementos (like postcards or pressed flowers) to remember each stop.

Pro Tip: Always check the duration of your stopover to ensure you return to the train on time—missing departure can disrupt your entire itinerary!

## 11.2 Top Stops on The Ghan: Alice Springs, Katherine Gorge, Uluru

The Ghan offers several incredible stopovers that showcase the heart of Australia. Here are three standout destinations:

**Alice Springs:**

- Explore the Royal Flying Doctor Service Museum to learn about healthcare in remote areas.
- Visit the Desert Park to see native animals and plants in recreated desert habitats.
- Take a hot air balloon ride at sunrise for panoramic views of the MacDonnell Ranges.

**Katherine Gorge (Nitmiluk National Park):**
- Cruise along the gorge's tranquil waters, surrounded by towering sandstone cliffs.
- Hike scenic trails like the Baruwei Loop Walk for stunning vistas.
- Opt for a helicopter flight to marvel at the labyrinthine system of gorges from above.

**Uluru (Ayers Rock):**
- Witness the rock's mesmerizing color changes during sunrise or sunset.
- Learn about Anangu culture at the Cultural Centre and take a guided walk around the base of Uluru.
- Stargaze under some of the clearest skies in the world with expert astronomers.

**Fun Fact:** Many Indigenous-led tours provide insights into Dreamtime stories connected to these sacred sites.

## 11.3 Indian Pacific Highlights: Broken Hill, Kalgoorlie, Avon Valley

The Indian Pacific crosses diverse landscapes, offering unique opportunities to explore mining heritage, wildflower country, and picturesque valleys. Don't miss these highlights:

Broken Hill:
- Discover the city's rich silver-mining history at the Sulphide Street Railway & Historical Museum.
- Visit Pro Hart Gallery to admire colorful artworks inspired by the Outback.
- Sample locally brewed craft beers at iconic pubs like The Palace Hotel.

Kalgoorlie:
- Tour the Super Pit, one of the largest open-cut gold mines in the world.
- Wander through historic streets lined with grand architecture from the gold rush era.
- Enjoy stargazing sessions away from city lights.

Avon Valley:
- Admire rolling hills dotted with wildflowers during spring.
- Go kayaking or fishing along the Avon River.

- Explore quaint towns like York, Western Australia's oldest inland settlement.

Insider Tip: Wildflower season (July–October) transforms Kalgoorlie and surrounding areas into a riot of colors.

## 11.4 Spirit of Queensland Gems: Daintree Rainforest, Great Barrier Reef

The Spirit of Queensland connects travelers with Tropical North Queensland's natural wonders. These two gems are not to be missed:

Daintree Rainforest:
- Walk along elevated boardwalks through ancient rainforest at Mossman Gorge.
- Spot cassowaries, tree kangaroos, and other rare wildlife on guided eco-tours.
- Take a dip in crystal-clear swimming holes or float down the Daintree River.

Great Barrier Reef:
- Snorkel or scuba Plunge among coral gardens teeming with marine life.

-Board a glass-bottom boat or semi-submersible vessel for non-swimmers to enjoy underwater views.
- Fly over the reef on a scenic helicopter tour for jaw-dropping aerial perspectives.

Pro Tip: Consider visiting Green Island or Fitzroy Island for day trips combining reef exploration with beach relaxation.

## 11.5 Guided Tours vs. Independent Exploration

Choosing between guided tours and independent exploration depends on your preferences and travel style:

Guided Tours:
- Pros: Expert guides share fascinating insights, pre-planned itineraries save time, and group logistics are handled for you.
- Cons: Less flexibility, potential crowds, and higher costs compared to DIY options.
- Best For: First-time visitors, those short on time, or anyone seeking hassle-free experiences.

Independent Exploration:

- Pros: Freedom to set your own pace, customize your itinerary, and avoid group dynamics.
- Cons: Requires more planning, navigation skills, and confidence in unfamiliar environments.
- Best For: Adventurous travelers, repeat visitors, or those who prefer solitude.

Hybrid Option: Combine both styles—for example, join a guided tour for key attractions and explore smaller towns independently.

## 11.6 Short Detours for Nature Lovers, Foodies, and History Buffs

Whether you're chasing waterfalls, savoring local flavors, or delving into Australia's past, here are ideas for quick yet rewarding detours:

For Nature Lovers:
- Hike to Florence Falls or Wangi Falls in Litchfield National Park near Darwin.
- Swim in the turquoise waters of Lake McKenzie on Fraser Island.
- Visit Cape Tribulation where rainforest meets reef.

For Foodies:

- Indulge in oysters and sparkling wine in Coffin Bay, South Australia.
- Sample fresh seafood platters at Port Douglas' waterfront restaurants.
- Pick tropical fruits straight from orchards in Cairns' hinterland.

For History Buffs:
- Step back in time at Sovereign Hill, an open-air museum recreating Victoria's gold rush days.
- Learn about Aboriginal rock art at Ubirr in Kakadu National Park.
- Explore Fremantle Prison, a UNESCO World Heritage Site, for tales of convicts and colonial life.

Pro Tip: Many train operators partner with local businesses to offer discounted rates on activities—check their websites for deals.

Final Thoughts

Off-train adventures turn a simple rail journey into a multi-dimensional experience, allowing you to connect deeply with Australia's people, places, and stories. Whether you're marveling at Uluru's spiritual aura, tasting Barossa Valley wines, or snorkeling in the Great Barrier Reef, every stop adds a new layer to your adventure.

## Chapter 12: Cultural Connections

Australia's railways don't just connect cities and landscapes—they also weave together the rich treasures of cultures that define this diverse nation. From learning about Indigenous traditions to celebrating regional arts, food, and festivals, rail travel offers countless opportunities to engage with Australia's vibrant heritage. In this chapter, we'll explore how to deepen your understanding of local cultures and forge meaningful connections along your journey.

## 12.1 Learning About Indigenous Australia Through Rail Travel

The history and culture of Australia's First Nations peoples are woven into the very fabric of the land—and train routes often pass through areas of profound spiritual significance. Here's how you can learn more about Indigenous Australia during your rail journey:

- Onboard Presentations: Many trains, such as The Ghan and Indian Pacific, feature onboard talks by

Indigenous guides or historians who share Dreamtime stories, traditional knowledge, and personal insights.
- Art Displays: Look out for exhibitions of Aboriginal art aboard luxury trains or at stations—these works often depict ancestral connections to the land.
- Excursions to Sacred Sites: Stopovers like Uluru, Katherine Gorge, and Kakadu National Park provide access to sites steeped in ancient lore, where guided tours reveal their cultural importance.

Pro Tip: Keep an open mind and heart when engaging with Indigenous history—it's a chance to reflect on the resilience and wisdom of Australia's original custodians.

## 12.2 Sacred Sites and Stories Along the Tracks

Australia is home to thousands of sacred sites that hold deep meaning for Indigenous communities. These places are not just landmarks; they're living embodiments of Dreamtime stories passed down over millennia. Here are some examples you might encounter along your route:

- Uluru (Ayers Rock): This massive sandstone monolith is central to Anangu creation myths and remains a site of immense spiritual power. Guided walks explain its significance and the protocols for respectful behavior.
- Kakadu National Park: Known for its stunning rock art galleries, Kakadu showcases centuries-old depictions of animals, spirits, and daily life from the Bininj/Mungguy people.
- Nitmiluk (Katherine Gorge): The Jawoyn people believe the gorge was carved by Bula, a creator spirit, and it continues to be a place of ceremony and storytelling.

Fun Fact: Some sacred sites have gender-specific restrictions—for example, certain areas may only be visited by women or men due to cultural protocols.

## 12.3 Respectful Engagement with Local Communities

When interacting with Indigenous communities, respect is paramount. Here's how to ensure your engagement is thoughtful and meaningful:

- Seek Permission: Always ask before taking photos of people, artwork, or sacred sites. Some areas prohibit photography altogether.
- Listen Actively: Whether attending a cultural performance or joining a guided tour, listen attentionsubscribe to what is being shared without interrupting or making assumptions.
- Support Ethical Tourism: Choose operators and experiences endorsed by Indigenous organizations, ensuring profits benefit local communities directly.
- Be Mindful of Language: Avoid using terms like "Aborigine," which many find outdated or offensive. Instead, refer to specific groups by their proper names (e.g., Arrernte, Yolngu).

Insider Tip: If unsure about appropriate behavior, simply ask politely—the majority of locals appreciate genuine curiosity and goodwill.

## 12.4 Meeting Fellow Travelers and Sharing Stories

One of the joys of rail travel is the opportunity to meet fellow passengers from all walks of life. Train journeys foster camaraderie, creating spaces where strangers become friends through shared experiences. Here's how to make the most of these interactions:

- Join Communal Spaces: Dining cars, observation decks, and lounges are perfect spots to strike up conversations over meals or drinks.
- Share Your Story: Talk about your own background, travels, and interests—it encourages others to open up too.
- Learn From Others: You might hear fascinating tales from seasoned adventurers, expats returning home, or locals sharing insider tips.
- Play Games Together: Card games, board games, or even trivia quizzes can break the ice and create lasting memories.

Pro Tip: Solo travelers often find train journeys particularly rewarding, as they naturally encourage socializing and forming bonds.

## 12.5 Celebrating Regional Cultures Through Food, Art, and Festivals

Each region of Australia has its own unique identity shaped by geography, history, and community. Rail travel lets you immerse yourself in these distinct flavors and traditions:

- Food:
- Sample bush tucker dishes made with native ingredients like wattleseed, finger limes, and kangaroo meat.
- Taste regional specialties such as Barossa Valley wines, Margaret River cheeses, and tropical fruits from Queensland.
- Attend farmers' markets or street food festivals to mingle with locals and try homemade delicacies.

- Art:
- Visit galleries showcasing contemporary Aboriginal art, such as those in Alice Springs or Cairns.
- Admire public murals and sculptures in urban centers like Melbourne's laneways or Perth's Elizabeth Quay.
-Purchase authentic souvenirs like hand-painted boomerangs, didgeridoos, or dot paintings to support artists.

Festivals:
- Experience Darwin Festival's multicultural performances under starry skies.
- Join Adelaide's WOMADelaide for global music acts and workshops.

- Celebrate quirky events like Birdsville Races in Outback Queensland or Targa Tasmania motorsport rally.

**Fun Fact:** Australia hosts over 300 annual festivals, ranging from highbrow arts celebrations to quirky small-town gatherings!

**Final Thoughts**

Cultural connections enrich any journey, transforming scenic views and historic landmarks into deeply personal experiences. By embracing Indigenous heritage, meeting fellow travelers, and celebrating regional diversity, you'll come away with a greater appreciation for Australia's soul and spirit.

# Chapter 13: Photography and Journaling on the Rails

Train travel offers endless opportunities to capture breathtaking moments and reflect on your journey. Whether you're an avid photographer, a budding writer, or simply someone who loves collecting mementos, this chapter will guide you through preserving the beauty, emotions, and stories of your rail adventure.

## 13.1 Capturing Stunning Photos from Moving Trains

Photographing from a moving train can be challenging but incredibly rewarding. Here's how to make the most of this unique perspective:

- **Stabilize Your Camera:** Use a tripod or rest your camera/phone against a stable surface (like the window ledge) to minimize blur caused by motion.

- Shoot in Burst Mode: This allows you to take multiple shots quickly, increasing the chances of capturing sharp images despite the train's movement.
- Focus on Foreground Elements: Incorporate objects like trees, fences, or rocks near the tracks to add depth and dynamism to your photos.
- Avoid Overexposure: Bright sunlight reflecting off landscapes can wash out colors; adjust exposure settings manually if possible.

Pro Tip: Sit on the side of the train facing the direction of travel for smoother shots with fewer obstructions.

## 13.2 Camera Settings for Shooting Through Windows

Shooting through train windows presents its own set of challenges, but with the right techniques, you can still achieve stunning results:

- Turn Off Flash: Flash reflections will ruin your shot when shooting through glass—always use natural light instead.
- Use Manual Focus: Autofocus often struggles with window glare; switch to manual focus to ensure clarity on distant subjects.

- **Minimize Reflections:** Wear dark clothing to reduce reflections, and position yourself close to the window without touching it.
- **Adjust ISO and Shutter Speed:** Increase ISO slightly for low-light conditions and use faster shutter speeds to counteract motion blur.
- **Polarizing Filter:** If using a DSLR or mirrorless camera, attach a polarizing filter to cut down on glare and enhance colors.

**Insider Tip:** Clean the window discreetly before shooting—dust and smudges can detract from even the most picturesque scenes.

## 13.3 Best Times of Day for Landscape Shots

Timing is everything when it comes to photography. The "golden hours" around sunrise and sunset provide soft, warm lighting that enhances landscapes dramatically:

- **Sunrise:** Early mornings offer crisp air, minimal crowds, and vibrant hues as the day begins. Capture dew-kissed foliage or mist rising from rivers.

- Sunset: Late afternoons bathe the land in golden tones, perfect for photographing red deserts, coastal cliffs, or lush rainforests.
- Blue Hour: Just before sunrise or after sunset, the sky takes on deep blues and purples, creating moody, atmospheric shots.

Fun Fact: During long journeys like The Ghan or Indian Pacific, you'll experience both sunrise and sunset over vastly different terrains—be ready to snap away!

## 13.4 Keeping a Travel Journal: Reflecting on Your Journey

A travel journal is more than just a record—it's a way to process your experiences, express gratitude, and relive memories later. Here's how to start yours:

- Daily Entries: Dedicate time each evening to jot down highlights, thoughts, and feelings from the day. Include details like conversations, meals, or unexpected surprises.
- Sketches and Notes: Even if you're not an artist, simple sketches of landscapes, station signs, or wildlife can add personality to your journal.

- Quotes and Observations: Write down interesting quotes from fellow travelers, guides, or books you read during the trip.
- Ticket Stubs and Mementos: Paste tickets, postcards, pressed flowers, or other keepsakes into your journal for a tactile reminder of your journey.

Pro Tip: Use prompts like "What surprised me today?" or "How did I feel seeing [landmark]?" to spark creativity if you're stuck.

## 13.5 Creating Memories That Last: Souvenirs and Keepsakes

Souvenirs are tangible reminders of your travels, evoking memories long after the journey ends. Here's how to choose meaningful items that tell your story:

- Local Art and Crafts: Purchase handmade goods like Aboriginal paintings, woven baskets, or boomerangs to support artisans and preserve cultural heritage.
- Regional Foods: Bring home jars of honey, bottles of wine, or packets of native spices to savor flavors from your trip.

- Photography Prints: Turn your favorite photos into prints, albums, or digital slideshows to share with friends and family.
- Personalized Items: Customize souvenirs like engraved keychains, custom maps, or journals with notes about where they were purchased.
- Natural Treasures: Collect small tokens like pebbles, leaves, or shells (where permitted) to remind you of specific locations.

Creative Idea: Create a scrapbook combining photos, written reflections, and small mementos for a multi-dimensional keepsake.

**Final Thoughts**

Photography and journaling allow you to document and cherish every aspect of your rail journey—from sweeping vistas and fleeting encounters to quiet moments of introspection. By capturing stunning images, reflecting thoughtfully, and curating meaningful souvenirs, you'll create a treasure trove of memories that last a lifetime.

## Chapter 14: Insider Tips for First-Time Rail Travelers

Commencing on your first Australian rail journey is an exciting adventure, but it can also come with its own set of challenges. From mastering train etiquette to staying comfortable during long rides, this chapter will equip you with practical advice to make your experience smooth, enjoyable, and memorable.

## 14.1 Train Etiquette: Dos and Don'ts for a Smooth Ride

Train travel has its own unspoken rules that ensure everyone enjoys the journey. Here's how to be a considerate passenger:

**Dos:**
- Respect Personal Space: Keep your belongings tidy and avoid sprawling into shared areas like aisles or lounges.

- **Be Quiet in Shared Spaces:** Use headphones for music/videos, and keep conversations at a moderate volume.
- **Greet Fellow Passengers:** A friendly smile or "hello" goes a long way in creating a welcoming atmosphere.
- **Follow Instructions:** Pay attention to safety briefings and announcements from staff—they're there to help.

**Don'ts:**
- **Don't Hog Amenities:** Limit your time in dining cars or bathrooms so others can use them too.
- **Avoid Strong Smells:** Refrain from eating pungent foods in close quarters—it can disturb fellow passengers.
- **Don't Block Windows:** If seated by the window, share the view with aisle passengers who want to take photos.
- **Refrain from Complaints:** Delays or minor inconveniences happen—stay patient and adaptable.

**Pro Tip:** Bring earplugs or noise-canceling headphones if you're sensitive to noise; they're lifesavers on busy trains.

## 14.2 Handling Challenges: Delays, Connectivity Issues, and More

Even the best-laid plans can encounter hiccups. Here's how to handle common challenges gracefully:

- Delays: Trains may occasionally run late due to weather, track maintenance, or other factors.
- Stay calm and use the extra time to relax, read, or chat with fellow passengers.
- Check real-time updates via apps or station announcements.
- Notify any onward connections (like flights or accommodations) about delays to avoid complications.

- Connectivity Issues: Remote areas often lack reliable internet or phone service.
- Download offline maps, eBooks, podcasts, or movies before departure.
- Carry a physical map or guidebook as a backup.
- Embrace the opportunity to disconnect and immerse yourself in the journey.

- Lost or Damaged Luggage: While rare, mishaps can occur.
- Label your bags clearly with contact information.

- Keep valuables like passports, wallets, and medications in your carry-on.
- Report issues immediately to onboard staff or station personnel.

Insider Tip: Pack snacks, water, and entertainment for unexpected delays—you'll thank yourself later!

## 14.3 Staying Healthy and Comfortable on Long Journeys

Long train journeys require preparation to stay energized, hydrated, and relaxed. Follow these tips to feel your best:

- Stay Hydrated: Bring a reusable water bottle and refill it regularly. Avoid excessive caffeine or alcohol, which can dehydrate you.
- Eat Light and Nutritious: Opt for balanced meals rich in protein, fiber, and healthy fats to sustain energy levels. Many trains offer onboard dining options featuring regional specialties.
- Move Regularly: Stretch your legs by walking through the train every hour or two to prevent stiffness. Simple stretches in your seat can also help.

- Dress in Layers: Temperatures inside trains can fluctuate, especially overnight. Wear breathable fabrics and pack a light jacket or scarf.
- Prioritize Sleep: Bring a travel pillow, eye mask, and earplugs to create a cozy sleep environment. Platinum and Gold Service cabins provide beds, while Economy passengers should bring neck pillows.

Pro Tip: Avoid heavy meals right before bedtime to ensure restful sleep.

## 14.4 Connecting with Locals and Making Friends

One of the joys of rail travel is meeting new people, whether they're locals, fellow travelers, or onboard staff. Here's how to forge meaningful connections:

-Start Conversations: Ask open-ended questions like "What brings you here?" or "Have you traveled this route before?" to spark dialogue.
- Join Group Activities: Participate in onboard events like wine tastings, storytelling sessions, or trivia games to bond with others.

- Engage with Staff: Train attendants and guides are often fountains of knowledge about the region—don't hesitate to ask questions.
- Share Meals: Dining cars are natural gathering spots. Strike up conversations over breakfast or dinner to learn about different perspectives.
- Respect Boundaries: Not everyone wants to socialize, so gauge cues like body language and tone to determine if someone prefers solitude.

Fun Fact: Many seasoned travelers find lifelong friendships—or even romance—on long-distance trains!

**Final Thoughts**

With these insider tips, you're well-prepared to navigate the nuances of rail travel like a pro. From practicing good etiquette and handling challenges calmly to prioritizing health and building connections, these strategies will enhance your overall experience. Remember, flexibility and a positive attitude are key to making the most of your journey.

## Chapter 15: Sustainable Travel by Rail

In an era of growing environmental awareness, sustainable travel has become a priority for many adventurers. Trains offer one of the most eco-friendly ways to explore Australia's vast and diverse landscapes while minimizing your impact on the planet. In this chapter, we'll delve into why rail travel is a green choice, how it supports local economies, and practical steps you can take to reduce your carbon footprint during your journey.

### 15.1 Why Trains Are an Eco-Friendly Choice

Trains are widely regarded as one of the most sustainable modes of transportation due to their efficiency and lower emissions compared to cars and planes. Here's why choosing rail travel aligns with eco-conscious values:

- Lower Carbon Emissions: Trains produce significantly fewer greenhouse gases per passenger kilometer than airplanes or private vehicles. For example, The Ghan emits about 90% less $CO_2$ per person than flying between Adelaide and Darwin.

-Energy Efficiency: Modern trains use advanced technologies like regenerative braking and electric power, which conserve energy and reduce reliance on fossil fuels.

- Reduced Traffic Congestion: By opting for trains over roads, you help alleviate traffic congestion and the associated pollution in urban areas.

- Minimal Land Impact: Rail networks require less land disruption compared to highways or airports, preserving natural habitats and ecosystems.

Pro Tip: Choose operators that prioritize sustainability initiatives, such as using renewable energy sources or implementing waste reduction programs.

## 15.2 Supporting Local Economies Through Rail Tourism

Rail tourism not only benefits travelers but also plays a vital role in supporting regional economies across Australia. Here's how your journey contributes positively:

-Boosting Small Businesses: Many train routes pass through rural towns where passengers stop to shop, dine, or stay overnight. This influx of visitors provides critical income for local businesses like cafes, hotels, and tour operators.
-Preserving Heritage Sites: Revenue generated from rail tourism often funds the maintenance and promotion of historic landmarks, national parks, and cultural sites along the routes.
- Employment Opportunities: Train operators, station staff, guides, and artisans all benefit from jobs created by rail tourism. By participating, you're helping sustain livelihoods in remote communities.
- Showcasing Indigenous Culture: Many rail journeys highlight Aboriginal art, storytelling, and traditions, ensuring these practices continue to thrive and reach wider audiences.

Fun Fact: Some regional festivals and markets rely heavily on tourists arriving by train—your visit could directly support these vibrant events!

## 15.3 Reducing Your Carbon Footprint While Exploring Australia

While trains are already a low-impact mode of transport, there are additional steps you can take to further minimize your environmental footprint during your Australian adventure:

- Pack Light: Heavier luggage increases fuel consumption, so pack only what you need. Opt for reusable items like water bottles, utensils, and shopping bags.
- Choose Eco-Friendly Accommodations: Stay at hotels, lodges, or campsites that prioritize sustainability practices, such as solar power, water conservation, and recycling programs.
- Offset Your Emissions: If your trip includes flights or car rentals, consider purchasing carbon offsets to balance out your overall impact. Many airlines and organizations offer verified offset programs.
- Support Green Operators: Look for rail companies that invest in renewable energy, eco-friendly amenities, or conservation efforts. For instance, some operators partner with wildlife sanctuaries or national parks to protect native species.
- Leave No Trace: Whether exploring national parks or visiting small towns, follow Leave No Trace principles—dispose of waste responsibly, respect wildlife, and avoid damaging natural or cultural sites.
- Eat Locally Sourced Food: Onboard meals and local eateries often feature ingredients sourced from nearby

farms, reducing the distance food travels and supporting sustainable agriculture.

Insider Tip: Bring a reusable coffee cup and snack containers to reduce single-use plastics during your journey.

Final Thoughts

Sustainable travel isn't just about reducing harm—it's about creating positive impacts for both people and the planet. By choosing rail travel, you're already making a responsible decision that supports cleaner air, thriving communities, and preserved landscapes. With mindful actions like packing sustainably, supporting local enterprises, and embracing eco-conscious habits, you can amplify the benefits of your journey.

As you reflect on this guidebook, remember that every step you take toward sustainable exploration helps safeguard Australia's incredible beauty for future generations. Thank you for being part of the solution—and happy, green travels!

## Chapter 16: Appendices

This chapter provides practical resources and tools to enhance your Australian rail journey. From apps and maps to glossaries and checklists, these appendices are designed to make planning and traveling seamless, enjoyable, and stress-free.

## 16.1 Appendix A: Apps, Websites, and Resources

Here's a curated list of essential digital tools and websites to help you plan, navigate, and maximize your rail adventure:

- Booking Platforms:
-Journey Beyond Rail Expeditions ([www.journeybeyondrail.com](http://www.journeybeyondrail.com))
-
QueenslandRailTravel([www.queenslandrailtravel.com](http://www.queenslandrailtravel.com))

- NSWTrainLink([www.transportnsw.info](http://www.transportnsw.info))

- Navigation Apps:
- Google Maps (for general navigation)
- Moovit (public transit schedules and routes)
- CityMapper (urban transport planner for cities like Sydney and Melbourne)

Travel Planning Tools:
- Rome2Rio (compare train, bus, and flight options)
- TripIt (organize itineraries and reservations in one place)
- Skyscanner or Kayak (find connecting flights if needed)

Weather and Safety:
- BOM Weather App (Bureau of Meteorology forecasts)
- Emergency+ App (Australia-wide emergency services locator)

Pro Tip: Download offline versions of maps and apps before departure, especially for remote areas with limited connectivity.

## 16.2 Appendix B: Glossary of Train and Rail Terminology

Understanding rail-specific terms can make your journey smoother. Here are some common phrases:

- Cabin: Private sleeping quarters on luxury trains like The Ghan or Indian Pacific.
- Berth: A bunk-style bed in shared accommodation on sleeper trains.
- Dining Car: A dedicated train carriage where meals are served.
-Observation Deck: An open or glass-enclosed area at the end of certain carriages for panoramic views.
- RailMotor: A self-propelled train used on regional routes, such as the Savannahlander.
- Track Gauge: The width between railway tracks; Australia has several gauges, including standard, narrow, and broad.

## 16.3 Appendix C: Glossary of Local Phrases

Australian slang adds color to your travels. Here's a quick guide to understanding locals:

- Arvo: Afternoon.

- Brekkie: Breakfast.
- Fair Dinkum: Genuine or true.
- G'day: Hello or good day.
- Maccas: McDonald's (a popular fast-food chain).
- No Worries: No problem or you're welcome.
- Tucker: Food.

Fun Fact: Australians love abbreviating words—don't be surprised if "barbecue" becomes "barbie"!

## 16.4 Appendix D: Detailed Maps of Major Train Routes

Detailed maps are invaluable for visualizing your journey. Below are descriptions of key routes included in this appendix:

- The Ghan: Adelaide → Alice Springs → Katherine → Darwin
- Indian Pacific: Sydney → Broken Hill → Adelaide → Kalgoorlie → Perth
- Spirit of Queensland: Brisbane → Rockhampton → Townsville → Cairns
- Overland: Melbourne ↔ Adelaide
- Savannahlander: Cairns → Forsayth

These maps highlight major stops, scenic highlights, and distances between destinations. You'll also find labeled national parks, rivers, and other points of interest.

## 16.5 Appendix E: Contact Information for Booking Operators and Emergency Contact Numbers

Having access to reliable contacts ensures peace of mind during your trip. Here's a breakdown of important numbers:

Train Operators:
- Journey Beyond Rail Expeditions: +61 8 8213 4400
- Queensland Rail Travel: +61 7 3606 4500
- NSW TrainLink: +61 2 8267 0000

Emergency Services:
- Police, Fire, Ambulance: 000 (Australia-wide emergency number)
- Non-Emergency Police Assistance: 131 444

- Tourism Hotlines:
- Tourism Australia: +61 2 9360 1111

- State-Specific Tourist Information Centers:
- NSW: 1300 362 052
- QLD: 1300 369 700
- VIC: 1800 819 903

Pro Tip: Save these numbers in your phone and write them down in case of battery failure.

## 16.6 Appendix F: Glossary of Rail Travel Terms

Expand your knowledge of rail travel jargon with this comprehensive glossary:

-All Aboard: Announcement signaling passengers to board the train.
- Conductor: Staff member responsible for managing onboard operations and assisting passengers.
- Crossing Loop: A section of track allowing trains traveling in opposite directions to pass safely.
-First Class: Premium seating or accommodation class offering extra comfort and amenities.
- Lounge Car: A casual space for relaxation, often featuring snacks, drinks, and seating.
- Rail Pass: A ticket allowing unlimited travel within a specified timeframe or network.

- Sleeper Service: Overnight trains equipped with sleeping facilities.

## 16.7 Appendix G: Checklist for Planning Your Rail Adventure

Use this checklist to ensure you've covered all bases before commencing on your journey:

Pre-Departure Planning:
-Research train routes and schedules.
-Book tickets and accommodations well in advance.
-Arrange visas (if applicable) and travel insurance.

Packing Essentials:
-Comfortable clothing suitable for varying climates.
-Reusable water bottle, snacks, and toiletries.
-Camera, chargers, and power bank.
-Earplugs, eye mask, and travel pillow (for Economy passengers).

Onboard Needs:
-Download entertainment (eBooks, podcasts, movies).
-Bring cash and cards for incidental expenses.
-Pack medications and copies of prescriptions.

**At Destinations:**
-Confirm onward transportation (taxis, shuttles, etc.).
-Research local attractions and dining options.
-Carry a small daypack for excursions.

**Pro Tip:** Double-check your packing list the night before departure to avoid last-minute stress.

**Final Thoughts**

The appendices in this chapter provide everything you need to confidently plan, execute, and enjoy your Australian rail adventure. Whether you're referencing detailed maps, brushing up on local slang, or consulting emergency contacts, these resources ensure you're prepared for whatever comes your way.

Thank you for joining us on this guide to exploring Australia by rail. May your journey be filled with breathtaking scenery, meaningful connections, and unforgettable memories. All aboard—and safe travels!

## Chapter 17: Index

**Quick Reference for Topics, Places, and Tips**

**A**
- Accommodation options: [Chapter- 7]
-Budget-friendlystays: [7.4]-budget-friendly-hostels-and-guesthouses
-Luxuryhotels: [7.1]-luxury-hotels-close-to-major-stations
-Uniquelodging: [7.5]-unique-lodging-experiences
-Adelaide: [9.4]-adelaide-wine-country-and-festivals-galore[16.4]-appendix-d-detailed-maps-of-major-train-routes
-AliceSprings: [9.8]-alice-springs-heart-of-the-red-centre[11.2]-top-stops-on-the-ghan-alice-springs-katherine-gorge-uluru
-Apps: [16.1]-appendix-a-apps-websites-and-resources

**B**
-Bookingtickets: [4.1]-step-by-step-guide-to-booking-tickets, [16.5]-appendix-e-contact-information-for-booking-operators-and-emergency-contact-numbers

-BrokenHill: [9.3]-brisbane-gateway-to-sunshine-and-surf, [11.3]-indian-pacific-highlights-broken-hill-kalgoorlie-avon-valley

C
-Cairns: [9.6]-cairns-tropical-paradise-and-reef-adventures, [11.4]-spirit-of-queensland-gems-daintree-rainforest-great-barrier-reef
-Camerasettings: [13.2]-camera-settings-for-shooting-through-windows
-Carbonfootprint: [15.3]-reducing-your-carbon-footprint-while-exploring-australia
-Culturalconnections: chapter-12-cultural-connections

D
-Darwin: [9.7]-darwin-outback-vibes-and-indigenous-culture, [16.4]-appendix-d-detailed-maps-of-major-train-routes
-Diningonboard: [5.3]-dining-cars-and-meals-on-board, [6.2]-highlights-from-the-ghans-outback-dinners

E
-Eco-friendlytravel: chapter-15-sustainable-travel-by-rail

-Emergencycontacts: [16.5]-appendix-e-contact-information-for-booking-operators-and-emergency-contact-numbers
-Excursions: chapter-11-off-train-adventures

F
-Foodandbeverages: chapter-6-culinary-delights-along-the-rails, [4.7]-food-and-beverage-expenses-onboard
-Festivals: [9.4]-adelaide-wine-country-and-festivals-galore, [12.5]-celebrating-regional-cultures-through-food-art-and-festivals

G
-Glossary: [16.2]-appendix-b-glossary-of-train-and-rail-terminology, [16.3]-appendix-c-glossary-of-local-phrases, [16.6]-appendix-f-glossary-of-rail-travel-terms
-Glamping: [7.6]-glamping-under-the-stars-near-uluru
- Great Barrier Reef: [11.4]-spirit-of-queensland-gems-daintree-rainforest-great-barrier-reef

H
-Heritagecottages: [7.7]-heritage-cottages-in-historic-towns-like-broken-hill
- Hotels near stations: [7.1]-luxury-hotels-close-to-major-stations

## I
-IndianPacific: [3.2]-indian-pacific-coast-to-coast-magic-between-sydney-and-perth, [16.4]-appendix-d-detailed-maps-of-major-train-routes
-Indigenousculture: [12.1]-learning-about-indigenous-australia-through-rail-travel, [12.2]-sacred-sites-and-stories-along-the-tracks

## K
-KakaduNationalPark: [11.3]-indian-pacific-highlights-broken-hill-kalgoorlie-avon-valley
-KatherineGorge: [11.2]-top-stops-on-the-ghan-alice-springs-katherine-gorge-uluru

## L
-Luxurytrains: [2.3]-luxury-trains-vs-budget-friendly-options, [4.6]-accommodation-classes-platinum-gold-economy
-Localphrases: [16.3]-appendix-c-glossary-of-local-phrases

## M
-Maps: [16.4]-appendix-d-detailed-maps-of-major-train-routes
-Melbourne: [9.2]-melbourne-culture-cafés-and-hidden-laneways, [16.4]-appendix-d-detailed-maps-of-major-train-routes

## N
-Navigationtype: chapter-8-transportation-beyond-trains, [16.1]-appendix-a-apps-websites-and-resources

## O
-Off-trail adventures: chapter-11-off-train-adventures
-Onlinereservations: [4.2]-online-reservations-vs-travel-agencies

## P
-Packingessentials: [4.8]-packing-essentials-for-long-train-rides), [16.7]-appendix-g-checklist-for-planning-your-rail-adventure
-Perth: [9.5]-perth-modern-meets-natural-beauty, [16.4]-appendix-d-detailed-maps-of-major-train-routes
-Photographytips: [13.1]-capturing-stunning-photos-from-moving-trains, [13.2]-camera-settings-for-shooting-through-windows

## Q
-QueenslandRail: [3.3]-spirit-of-queensland-tropical-beauty-from-brisbane-to-cairns, [16.5]-appendix-e-contact-information-for-booking-operators-and-emergency-contact-numbers

**R**
-Resources: [16.1]-appendix-a-apps-websites-and-resources
-Railterminology: [16.2]-appendix-b-glossary-of-train-and-rail-terminology, [16.6]-appendix-f-glossary-of-rail-travel-terms

**S**
-Scenichighlights: chapter-10-scenic-highlights-along-the-way
- Spirit of Queensland: [3.3]-spirit-of-queensland-tropical-beauty-from-brisbane-to-cairns, [16.4]-appendix-d-detailed-maps-of-major-train-routes
-Sydney: [9.1]-sydney-coastal-charm-and-urban-energy, [16.4]-appendix-d-detailed-maps-of-major-train-routes

**T**
-TheGhan: [3.1]-the-ghan-from-adelaide-to-darwin-the-ultimate-outback-adventure, [16.4]-appendix-d-detailed-maps-of-major-train-routes
-Trainetiquette: [14.1]-train-etiquette-dos-and-don'ts-for-a-smooth-ride
-Traveljournaling: [13.4]-keeping-a-travel-journal-reflecting-on-your-journey

**U**

-Uluru: [11.2]-top-stops-on-the-ghan-alice-springs-katherine-gorge-uluru, [7.6]-glamping-under-the-stars-near-uluru

**V**
-Vegan/vegetarianoptions: [6.9]-special-dietary-needs-vegan-vegetarian-and-gluten-free-options

**W**
-Wildlifespotting: [10.5]-wildlife-spotting-opportunities
-Wineregions: [6.7]-barossa-valley-wines-indian-pacific, [9.4]-adelaide-wine-country-and-festivals-galore

This index provides a quick way to navigate this book's content, ensuring you can easily find information on specific topics, places, or tips. Happy travels!

## Chapter 18: Conclusion: All Aboard for Adventure

As we reach the final stop on this literary journey through Australia by rail, it's clear that train travel is far more than a mode of transportation—it's an invitation to explore, connect, and discover. From the rugged Outback landscapes of The Ghan to the lush rainforests along the Spirit of Queensland, each route tells a story as vast and varied as the continent itself. Whether you're marveling at sunrise over Uluru, savoring Barossa Valley wines, or meeting fellow travelers in a cozy dining car, every moment aboard Australia's railways becomes part of your own unique narrative.

This guide has equipped you with everything you need to plan and embrace your rail adventure—from booking tickets and packing essentials to capturing memories and reducing your carbon footprint. Along the way, we've celebrated the beauty of slow travel, the joy of cultural connections, and the importance of sustainability. By choosing trains, you're not only experiencing Australia in its purest form but also contributing to a greener future for generations to come.

Remember, the magic of rail travel lies not just in the destinations but in the journey itself—the rhythmic clatter of wheels, the ever-changing scenery outside your window, and the unexpected encounters that remind us of our shared humanity. So whether you're chasing sunsets over the Nullarbor Plain, snorkeling in the Great Barrier Reef, or glamping under starlit skies near Alice Springs, let curiosity be your compass and wonder be your guide.

Thank you for joining us on this unforgettable ride. May your adventures across Australia's rails leave you inspired, enriched, and eager to return again and again. Until then, keep dreaming of distant horizons, new friendships, and the endless possibilities that await when you step aboard.

All aboard—and may your travels be filled with joy, discovery, and countless stories worth telling.

Printed in Dunstable, United Kingdom